DISTRICT 3
BATTLE OF THE BANDS

TINA CAMPANELLA

JOHN BLAKE

Published by John Blake Publishing Ltd,
3 Bramber Court, 2 Bramber Road,
London W14 9PB, England

www.johnblakepublishing.co.uk

www.facebook.com/Johnblakepub   facebook

twitter.com/johnblakepub   twitter

First published in paperback in 2013

ISBN: 978-1-78219-361-6

British Library Cataloguing-in-Publication Data:

A catalogue record for this book is available from the British Library.

Design by www.envydesign.co.uk

Printed in Great Britain by CPI Group (UK) Ltd

1 3 5 7 9 10 8 6 4 2

Papers used by John Blake Publishing are natural, recyclable products made
from wood grown in sustainable forests. The manufacturing processes
conform to the environmental regulations of the country of origin.

Every attempt has been made to contact the relevant copyright-holders,
but some were unobtainable. We would be grateful if the
appropriate people could contact us.

DISTRICT 3

BATTLE OF
THE BANDS

Tina Campanella is a former tabloid and magazine journalist. You can tweet her at @littlebell1982

CONTENTS

DISTRICT 3

CHAPTER ONE

FROM WEST END TO *X FACTOR*

They may not have made it through to the final of *X Factor* 2012, but there's no disguising how popular District 3 have become. Favourites of both their fellow *X Factor* contestants and the audience at home, even their greatest rivals, Josh, JJ, Jaymi and George from Union J, were weeping when the boys were eliminated in Week Six of the live shows.

It was a shock for everyone to see them go, especially after they'd given what everyone agreed had been their best performance of the season.

Sweet and funny, Greg, Dan and Mickey scored themselves a legion of fans – who call themselves '3eeks' – from the moment they appeared at their first *X Factor* audition. And the love just kept coming! By the end of the competition they had more than 350,000 followers from all over the world on Twitter and that number grows daily.

Watching them lark about with each other, we were won over by their close friendship and amazing harmonies, not to mention their dashing looks! What's not to like about this gorgeous trio?

The Battle of the Bands was fought over six long weeks of live *X Factor* showdowns. And week after week, the battle constantly changed direction.

One week, District 3 would emerge victorious, before Union J would stage an entertaining comeback the next. Greg, Dan and Mickey would then fight back so hard and so impressively that the Union J boys were convinced they were going home. On and on it went, a fight so close it was impossible to call. However, there could only be one winner in the boy band war, and the country was just about torn in two deciding who that should be.

But as you're about to find out, these three boys began their fight for fame long before the *X Factor*. Each of the lads had been working towards their collective stardom from the moment they could walk and talk.

Becoming District 3 and storming the music world was something the lads were just born to do. All their friends and families knew they had star potential, and it didn't take long for the *X Factor* judges to see it either.

They've been likened to JLS and One Direction and with their fresh and soulful sound, who knows how far their star will rise? One thing's for sure: District 3 have a long and exciting career to look forward to, and we can't wait to see what they do next! Ups and downs, highs and lows… it's all here in this revealing book about your favourite new band.

This is District 3's story so far.

CHAPTER TWO

GMD3'S FIRST AUDITION

Outside the O2 Arena, the sun was shining on the thousands of hopefuls who had turned up to try out at the *X Factor* auditions. Host Dermot O'Leary was walking through the crowds outside, chatting to a few random auditionees, when he came across three strikingly handsome boys in T-shirts.

They had warm smiles and something about them seemed special, so he began chatting to them. They introduced themselves as GMD3 and at first Dermot struggled to repeat the name.

'G-M-D-3,' he said, carefully. 'Why are you called that?'

'It's our initials,' laughed one band member, who was wearing a cap. 'This is Greg, Mickey and I'm Dan,' he told Dermot, introducing himself and his friends.

'We get mixed up a lot,' explained Greg, joining in the

conversation before he began reeling off a list of names they'd been mistakenly called in the past, including GHD and GMC.

Everyone laughed.

Eager to make an impression, they told Dermot that they'd known each other since school and had begun to put the band together 18 months before.

'It started from nothing really serious,' said Mickey. 'Then all of a sudden it turned, er...'

'Serious?' interrupted Dan, and they all started to chuckle again. The boys had a warmth that made them instantly likeable and it was obvious they were great mates, but being nice isn't enough to win *The X Factor* and Dermot would have to wait until they got on stage to see if there was anything more to this cheerful threesome than their sunny dispositions.

After waiting for hours, it was finally their turn to sing. They'd been rehearsing like mad and they hoped that they were good enough to impress the judges. With determined looks on their faces, they strode confidently onto the glitzy stage.

With their family backstage to cheer them on, they yelled: 'Hello, London!' before making their way to the middle, where they found themselves smack-bang in front of Louis Walsh, Tulisa Contostavlos, Nicole Scherzinger and Gary Barlow.

Mickey was grinning from ear to ear when he saw the huge crowds. He loved being in front of an audience and this was the biggest he'd ever seen.

'Hello, guys,' said Gary, in an effort to stop the distracting cheers from behind him. 'Where do you rehearse?'

Greg replied: 'Mickey lives in Windsor with his parents, and me and Dan just got a flat up there.'

'So this is full-time, you're serious about this?' he asked.

'Yes,' they all chorused.

Gary took a moment to look impressed at their dedication, before asking what they were going to sing.

Greg revealed it would be the Boyz II Men classic, 'I'll Make Love To You', and from the sounds of the cheers, the audience definitely approved of their choice.

Nicole immediately perked up, drawling: 'Bring it on!'

There was quite a pause before they began. It felt like all three boys wanted to savour the moment, soaking it up in case it was their only opportunity.

'Close your eyes, make a wish…' Dan began softly, melting hearts everywhere, before the other two boys joined in.

Girls in the audience began to blush, as if the song's words were being sung directly to them. One girl whispered to another: 'They're really good, aren't they?'

And she wasn't the only one who was thinking it.

Gary smiled kindly at them, as the boys ramped up the power in their voices. Growing in confidence before the audience's very eyes, they quickly got into the zone and soon impressed the judges with every note they sang.

In the audience, people were standing and swaying their arms from side to side, joined by Nicole, who waved an imaginary lighter in the air in a show of appreciation. Even Tulisa's eyes widened with surprise – some would say she was even blushing.

When they finished their soulful rendition the audience erupted into cheers and screams. As huge grins spread across their faces, it was obvious the boys were pleased with how their performance had gone and relieved it was over!

Unable to control the crowds, the judges decided that if

they couldn't beat them, they'd join them. Starting with Tulisa, they all stood up and clapped.

Greg patted his chest to try and calm his nerves as Gary took control of the situation. 'I've got a feeling you're going to need to get used to this,' he said, about the obvious female attention they were getting.

'This is what we've been looking for,' said Louis, who was definitely excited. 'I feel the same way about this band as when I first saw JLS.'

It was high praise indeed and exactly what the boys must have dreamed they'd hear.

'Not only are you a good-looking band,' Tulisa added, 'but your vocals are so on point.'

'You all rehearsed yourselves, you prepared yourselves and you guys were ready,' said Nicole. 'All you needed was the opportunity, and this was your opportunity.'

It was as if the American R&B star had read their minds; it was definitely the chance they'd been waiting for. Deep down, something had told them that they were good enough for the competition. Now the judges were telling them the same thing.

'Guys, that really was a terrific audition,' said Gary, summing it up. 'Individually, your voices are excellent but when you blend them together it's like listening to one sound. It is absolutely gorgeous – it's so exciting to see this.'

The votes were an obvious formality and everyone on the panel gave them a resounding 'Yes!'

The boys would keep the judges' words in their hearts for the tough times that would surely lie ahead but for now, they were through to Bootcamp. And on that day, it was all they had hoped for.

Hugging each other tightly, they left the stage to celebrate the start of their *X Factor* journey. But although it was the first time that Britain had really taken notice of the threesome, their journey actually started a long time before 2012.

CHAPTER THREE

DISTRICT 3 ~
FRIENDS FOR LIFE

MICKEY CURTIS PARSONS

QUICK FACTS:
Date of Birth: 25/8/94
Born: Nuneaton, Warwickshire
Parents: Carol and Steve Parsons
Siblings: Matthew
Grew Up: Cleethorpes
Schools: Cloverfields Primary, Humberston; Windsor Boys School

Mickey Parsons' mum always knew that he was going to be a star. She had seen the signs from a very early age. At the age of just three, she would close the curtains and Mickey would perform a dance with his brother, Matthew.

His mum Carol had been in an ABBA tribute band and certainly knew a thing or two about performing. It was as if young Mickey was practising for the time when, 15 years later, he would appear on one of the country's biggest stages. The toddler would regularly send his family into hysterics by performing what Carol describes as a 'jiggle'.

She told the *Grimsby Telegraph*: 'Mickey was a really, really cute baby and I'm not surprised he is on stage now because I always knew there was a spark in him. When he was little, he used to walk in the room and do a little "jiggle" – I can't describe it, it was like a little salsa dance.

'He used to have a massive grin on his face and say "helloooo" and walk back out of the room.'

And it wasn't just the family who were amused by the young boy, Mickey was used to entertaining strangers, too.

'He's a perfectionist – when I used to perform on stage, Mickey always used to sneak on and straighten my microphone wire – it used to make the audience laugh,' Carol said.

While at Humberston's Cloverfields Primary School, he appeared in a musical version of *Robin Hood*, in which he took the lead role. As part of his preparation, he got his grandmother Patricia to film him prancing about on the roof of her house, using a video camera he was given as a present. His gran was terrified he might hurt himself, so she refused to allow him to climb up high but although he hadn't been able to do the performance he had wanted, this demonstrated to his family how keen he was to do whatever it takes to succeed in showbusiness!

The first time his mum knew he had real talent was when his brother entered a talent competition at Butlins in Skegness. Matthew lost his nerve at the last minute, but

Mickey was keen to take his place. Carol hid under a table, terrified her son would make a fool of himself as he didn't know the words to any songs but Mickey sang a Westlife song perfectly and according to his mother, 'took control of the stage'.

After his talent was revealed, he joined The Stagecoach Theatre Group, based at The Lindsey School in Cleethorpes. After being awarded a half-scholarship, he was able to pursue his interest in acting and singing. Later, Mickey went to the Napa Dance School in Hull, where he was given tap dancing lessons from the renowned teacher, Bev Wade.

With a newfound confidence, he was ready to take on the world of showbiz and was propelled to national stardom at the age of eleven with his first attempt at the big time. Fox Kids TV had teamed up with the supermarket Asda and the biscuit maker Jammie Dodgers, for a programme called *Jam On The Mic*. Mickey's mum entered him at his local store and after he won the first few rounds, he was one of only ten children who were rushed down to London's famous Abbey Road studios to make a professional recording.

Mickey sang Mariah Carey's hit 'Hero' and the baby-faced boy went down a storm with viewers of the programme as he belted out the number. Thrusting his arms about, he delivered a passionate performance, prompting presenter Emma Fairclough to say: 'You superstar! You were rocking that, weren't you?'

Soon after, he auditioned for and won the chance to appear in the first modern run of *The Sound of Music*. The musical was being staged by Sir Andrew Lloyd Webber, who had found his leading lady courtesy of a reality TV programme: *How Do You Solve A Problem Like Maria?*

Mickey played the part of Kurt, alongside his later

bandmate Greg West, who played another of the Von Trapp children, Friedrich. Before he knew it, he was treading the boards of one of the most famous stages in the world, the London Palladium.

With Mickey appearing regularly on stage in London, in 2006 the family moved from Cleethorpes to Windsor in order to help him further his acting career. The move to the edge of Britain's capital city allowed him to attend the prestigious Sylvia Young Theatre School in London, about twenty miles from their new home. Others who have attended the school include Spice Girl Emma Bunton and pop star Eliza Doolittle. It was while studying at Sylvia Young's that he met the third youngster who would later become his bandmate: Dan.

The start of the boys' pop career would have to wait, though as Mickey suffered a setback when he was forced to move to Windsor Boys School because his parents couldn't afford the fees for the exclusive and expensive private theatre school. Having struck up such a good friendship, Mickey made sure he stayed in touch with Greg and Dan, however.

About two years later, he was sitting with his two friends on a bench outside London's Marylebone station, about a mile away from the theatre school, when he played them some songs he had written at home. Greg and Dan thought the songs were amazing and suddenly the idea was born – they would form a band.

That night they all got together at Mickey's house for a sleep over and drew up plans for their assault on the pop world. And so GMD3, which would later become District 3, was formed, and Mickey was just a step away from becoming the nation's heartthrob we know and love today.

GREG WEST

QUICK FACTS:

Date of Birth: 22/7/94
Born: Essex
Parents: Stuart and Tracey West
Sister: Olivia
Grew Up: Harwich, Essex
Schools: Chase Lane Primary, Harwich; Manningtree High School

The main guitarist of the group, Greg West, was one of those youngsters who begin showing their musical potential from an early age.

Greg's first school was Chase Lane Primary, where his singing talent was spotted by the staff when he was only in Year Five. His Year Six teacher, Jude Nash, has told the *Frinton Gazette*: 'We noticed he could sing when he was in Year Five. All of the children were asked to showcase a talent they had and he started to sing.

'In the Year Six Christmas performance I asked him to sing the song "Circle Of Life" from *The Lion King* and he shone. After that, any opportunity for an individual performance, we gave to him.'

The Essex boy always jumped at the chance to have his time on stage but shone in other subjects at the school, too. Another teacher, Mrs Nash, said he was good at all his subjects and was a superb footballer as well.

Although he had shown early promise, it was only at secondary school that he really began to blossom into the superstar he would eventually become. Just a year after starting Manningtree High School in Essex, Greg scored a part in the first re-run of *The Sound of Music* on the West End stage. Unlike many musicals that feature children in the main roles, the youngsters in *The Sound of Music* are major parts, the sort that could be intimidating for any young up-and-coming actors.

Greg scored the part of Friedrich, one of the Von Trapp children. Because he was only twelve at the time, he had to share the role with two other children of a similar age, who took it in turns to appear on stage. Also appearing in the same show was his later bandmate Mickey Parsons, who had won the part of Kurt Von Trapp.

The lead part of Maria was found by a TV talent show and had Greg followed it, this would have given him a taste of what was to come. Week in, week out, Connie Fisher battled it out for a whole autumn until she finally ended up winning the chance to appear in the top London production and went on to be seen by tens of thousands of fans.

How Do You Solve A Problem Like Maria?, as the show was called, was the first of its kind on the BBC and was an attempt to take on ITV in the main Saturday night primetime slot against its popular singing programme, *The X Factor*.

On Christmas Eve 2006, Greg and other cast members performed a medley of songs from the show as part of The Royal Variety Performance at the London Coliseum in front of HRH Prince Charles and the Duchess of Cornwall. You can also hear his voice on the album subsequently produced, which featured the soundtrack of the hit show. It was a major accolade to be chosen – he was the only one out of the three child actors who played Friedrich to have his voice recorded for the album.

With London just a stone's throw away from his home, unlike his bandmate Mickey, Greg's family didn't immediately have to move further south for him to carry on performing. As a result, he was at first able to stay in North Essex, where he carried on improving his skills by attending local theatre and dance schools.

In Clacton-on-Sea, he went to the Tiffany Stage School and later to The Company, another Clacton theatre school. But as a serious career in the theatre or music industry beckoned, his family decided it was important for him to follow his dreams and get the stage training he needed. As a result, he went to join one of the most famous stage schools in the country, the Sylvia Young School in London.

Soon after joining in 2007, he met and began performing with fellow pupils Mickey Parsons and Dan Ferrari-Lane, but it would be some time before they became the tight-knit unit we know and love today.

In 2009, Greg was still keen to get some solo exposure so entered several singing competitions, including Festival4stars. The event was a singing competition supported by Duncan James from Blue and TV presenter and former Eurovision Song Contest winner Cheryl Baker.

Greg sang another Mariah Carey song, 'When You Believe', and made it through to the national final before eventually being narrowly beaten by another singer. Inspired by his success, he, Mickey and Dan decided to turn their friendship into a proper band. By the time they left school, they had become the act that went on to audition at *X Factor*, calling themselves GMD3, after their initials Greg, Mickey and Dan. Within a few months they had managed to get a record deal, with the same label as The Wanted. In the run-up to their *X Factor* auditions, they played a string of venues around the South of England, before taking the chance to appear on the biggest stage of their lives – *The X Factor*.

DAN FERRARI-LANE

QUICK FACTS:
Date of Birth: 7/4/93
Born: Wales
Father: Giancarlo Ferrari-Lane
Siblings: Caris
Grew Up: Porthcawl, Wales
Schools: Nottage Primary, Porthcawl Comprehensive, Sylvia Young Theatre School

Although he showed an early interest in performing, if it hadn't been for his determination to follow his dreams all the way to the bright lights of London, Dan Ferrari-Lane may never have shown *The X Factor* the talented singer he truly was.

Despite not being picked to play the lead roles in the local shows he took part in as a youngster, he definitely had something that could be nurtured into that 'wow' factor. It was this 'something special' that won him so many fans from the moment he appeared on the 2012 *X Factor* show.

As well as appearing in several school productions, he also attended the Bridgend Youth Theatre when he was in his early teens. One of the directors, Roger Burnell, later told his local paper – *Wales News* – that he could see that Dan definitely had what it takes to be a star, even at such an early age.

Mr Burnell said: 'He always had a lot of charisma and was very natural. Even at that young age he played a lead role in front of 30 or 40 people in the crew and he dealt with that easily and confidently.'

One of the first major productions he appeared in, and one

which showed him what it was like to be in the limelight, was for his high school – Porthcawl Comprehensive – soon after making the step up from Nottage Primary. Being the main high school in the South Wales town, Porthcawl Comp put on a production that was staged every year in the busy sea-front theatre.

On 31 January 2007, 13-year-old Dan stepped out as one of the company in the school's production of *Return to the Forbidden Planet*. For four nights the Grand Pavilion echoed to the sounds of Dan and his friends performing rock and roll numbers like 'Great Balls Of Fire' and 'The Monster Mash'. At the heart of the story was a tussle between a hero space captain, a monster and a mad scientist, who has created a mysterious 'X Factor' potion which alters people's minds!

It seemed that Dan's first brush with the 'X Factor' had left him hooked on singing onstage because he quickly signed up to take part in the next available musical – Bridgend County Youth Theatre's lavish 2007 production of *West Side Story*. In this, he was alongside not just his starry-eyed schoolmates but everyone from the area where he lived, who was keen to try their hand at performing.

Dan needn't have worried about whether he would be able to compete, though as the production was a resounding success, winning rave reviews in the local press and prompting *Wales News* to say: 'What a show!' In it, he played one of the 'Jets' – a group who do battle with the rival group 'Sharks' in the back streets of 1950s New York.

While his heart was in Wales, Dan knew that he was never going to achieve the level of stardom that he sought if he chose to stay in his beloved country. Convinced he needed the kind of training that would take him to the top, he begged his parents to send him to stage school, far away in

London. At the age of fourteen, having attended Porthcawl Comprehensive for just a few years, he moved to London to attend the Sylvia Young Theatre School.

The move paid off. Within a few months he had successfully auditioned for a part in the musical *Oliver!*, alongside *Mr Bean* actor Rowan Atkinson and reality show *I'd Do Anything* winner, Jodie Prenger. As the cast were preparing for their West End run in 2008, Dan was one of the young actors from the show who appeared on BBC1 for their Children in Need appeal, singing the show's classics 'Food, Glorious Food' and 'Consider Yourself'. Blessed with youthful looks, he was able to appear as a much younger boy, despite being fifteen at the time.

It was at Sylvia Young that he met Greg and Mickey. One year older than the other two, he was in a different year group, so he was friendly with a slightly older crowd as well including Nathan Sykes from The Wanted. Nathan, whose band leapt into the charts in 2010, helped the boys out by giving them support on his Twitter page before they took part in the *X Factor* auditions.

Dan spotted in Mickey and Greg two boys he could work with, and so they all formed the band that became GMD3. As they grew more serious, he even turned down the chance to work for Disney in order to realise his dreams with his two best mates.

He made one attempt at individual success in 2010, when he entered Tesco's 1click2fame and although his performance later proved popular with fans, he didn't make it through to the final.

In the same year the band were picked up by the creator of The Saturdays and The Wanted, Jayne Collins, who began stirring up the kind of industry gossip that a new band needs.

DISTRICT 3

Although they didn't make it into the charts, they quickly developed a small and loyal fan base. It was only a matter of time before they were heading for huge success.

CHAPTER FOUR

BOOTCAMP ~ DISTRICT 3 VS UNION J

They don't call it Bootcamp for fun – it's really an exhausting and stressful process. Watching at home it sometimes looked as if the contestants were a bit too overemotional. Forgotten lyrics, panic over song choices… they were bursting into tears so often that staff had to keep tissues at the ready but they had good reason to have a bit of a cry.

'It's going to be the toughest 72 hours of the contestants' lives,' boomed the announcer when the first part of the series was broadcast in September 2012.

And, of course it was.

A staggering 211 auditionees were put through to the *X Factor's* 2012 Bootcamp, which for the first time ever took place outside of London because the Olympics were being held in the capital. Instead, Bootcamp's new home was The

UNION J AND DISTRICT 3: BATTLE OF THE BANDS

Echo Arena in Liverpool and took three July days to complete. But on the very first day, the judges reviewed the audition tapes and sent home 70 of the acts before they even sang a note! Imagine that – as an aspiring singer, you're told that you're through to the *X Factor* Bootcamp, you start to dream about your future but before you can truly shine, you're literally 'booted' off! Following this, the remaining contestants were then put into groups to take part in a sing-off. They could choose to perform from the following songs:

'Stronger (What Doesn't Kill You)'
'Respect'
'Moves Like Jagger'
'Are You Gonna Go My Way'
'Crazy In Love'
'Next To Me'
'She Said'
'Use Somebody'
'How To Save A Life'

After each performance the judges decided which acts to keep and which ones to eliminate. Eventually, the final 25 were told they were going to Judges' Houses. On the second day, those who were left had to each perform one song in front of a live audience. They then spent a restless night waiting for the judges to decide who would go on to the next exciting stage. No wonder they say not everyone can take it!

One by one, the number of acts dwindled.

In those three days, some dreams were dashed and for others, they came true. Many went home sobbing, to be comforted by friends and family – including George Shelley, who had met Triple J at the event, where they'd all become firm friends.

But the judges had one more decision to make and it was to prove a tough one. There was one spot left for the Judges' Houses stage – and two bands wanted to fill it. Both were obviously talented and included good-looking lads in their line-ups. It would all come down to a sing-off between GMD3 and Triple J.

The two bands were told they were going head to head in front of the judges and they knew that they would had to give the performance of their lives. They all stood on the stage, separated by a wide gulf. GMD3 had their arms around each other, and so did Triple J. Each of the bands appeared anxious as Gary said: 'Okay guys, the only way of settling this is to battle it out. We want to hear you sing again.'

With no backing music, they had just one minute to decide what they would sing and who would sing which part. Each group huddled together, whispering and practising their tunes. GMD3 were heard discussing their strategy. 'Let's keep it short,' said Mickey Parsons, 'because they're going to do more,' he added, referring to their rivals.

'Okay, guys, this is it,' Gary interrupted, and they knew it was now or never.

'Triple J, can you go first?' he asked, in a kindly voice. The boys nodded in reply. He wished them luck and they began to sing. As they listened, GMD3 looked nervous – even they could hear how good the song was. It was definitely going to be a hard act to beat. As Jaymi Hensley hit his band's last note, Gary thanked them all and they held each other tight. Then they waited patiently for their rivals to perform.

'Okay, guys,' Gary said to GMD3. 'Are you ready?'

Mickey looked to the skies for strength, while the others forced a smile and said that yes, they were ready.

Singing 'Bless The Broken Road', the boys put heart and soul into their performance. They sounded slightly less nervous than Triple J, but that might have been because they had gone second and so they had that little bit of extra time to calm themselves down.

Tulisa smiled at them, and Louis grinned from ear to ear as their voices boomed around the arena. It was beautiful and Triple J looked crestfallen, but no one could decide who had the edge. The judges huddled together to deliberate, speaking in hushed tones.

'This is tough, they both did so good,' said Nicole.

'It's very close, there's not much between them,' said Gary, knitting his brow in concentration. It was an important decision and not one to be taken lightly.

On stage, the boys took deep breaths as the judges continued to decide their fate. Greg put his arms around Dan and Mickey, and they all looked to the ground, making silent wishes. Finally, Gary began to speak. 'Okay, guys, you've been neck and neck throughout this competition and I'm sorry it's come down to this,' he started, 'but we've got to pick one of you right now.'

He paused and both the bands held their breath.

'The act taking the last place at the Judges' Houses is… GMD3.'

Closing their eyes in relief, the GMD3 boys mouthed a silent 'yes!' before going straight over to the devastated Triple J trio to console them.

'Congratulations, guys,' said Gary, as the boys all embraced. GMD3 had won the first round of the Battle of the Bands and as they walked offstage they could hardly bring themselves to smile, they were so overawed.

'What a way to get through to Judges' Houses, boys,' said Dermot O'Leary as he greeted them.

Still shocked, they began shaking their heads in disbelief and Greg said it was the hardest thing they'd ever had to do. But suddenly they realised they *had* got through and began yelling and punching the air in delight.

It had been an emotional day for both bands, but what no one could have predicted was what would come next. Because when GMD3 arrived in Vegas for the Judges' Houses stage, they were surprised to see four familiar faces there, too – Triple J's JJ, Jaymi and Josh, along with young George Shelley!

As it turned out, the band Rough Copy, who had also made it through Bootcamp, had a problem with one of their visas and so they couldn't fly to the US. And so they were out, and to replace them, Louis made a very clever decision – to invite Triple J back, and to persuade the extremely cute George Shelley to join them. Now called Union J, they would be GMD3's greatest rivals in the months ahead.

GMD3 had beaten them once – but could they do so again?

DID YOU KNOW?
Greg stands at 5ft 10in tall, while Dan is 5ft 8in.

Let's pause here and take a look at who made it through Bootcamp…

MENTOR: NICOLE SCHERZINGER (BOYS)

JAHMENE DOUGLAS
Fact: Jahmene lives at home with his mum, stepdad, two brothers and sister.

NATHAN FAGAN-GAYLE

Fact: In 2008, Nathan entered the *Big Brother: Celebrity Hijack* house. He came sixth on the show.

JAKE QUICKENDEN

Fact: Jake was extremely proud that his brother, Olly, got to see him perform at the auditions because sadly, he died of cancer just a few months later.

ADAM BURRIDGE

Fact: Adam is scared of statues – how weird is that?

JAMES ARTHUR

Fact: James loves watching women's beach volleyball, but what guy doesn't?

RYLAN CLARK

Fact: Rylan would love to enter the Eurovision Song Contest for Great Britain.

MENTOR: TULISA CONTOSTAVLOS (GIRLS)

JADE ELLIS

Fact: Jade has a huge crush on judge Nicole Scherzinger!

AMY MOTTRAM

Fact: Amy would love her mum to audition for *The X Factor* next year.

LUCY SPRAGGAN

Fact: Lucy was a massive N-Dubz fan when she was younger.

LEANNE ROBINSON

Fact: Aged just nine, Leanne was the youngest member of the adult choir at her church.

ELLA HENDERSON

Fact: At her first audition, Ella reduced the judges to tears when she sang her own song, 'Missed', and dedicated it to her late grandfather.

JADE COLLINS

Fact: At her audition Jade was praised by the guest judge Anastacia, who said she had a very emotional voice.

MENTOR: LOUIS WALSH (GROUPS)

MITSOTU (HOLLY COOPER, JAMES COLLINS AND JIMMY ESSEX)

Fact: James won the US televised competition, *Dirty Dancing*!

DUKE (MARKO PANDAZIS, EDWARD TRAVERS AND FLYNN STRONACH)

Fact: The beatboxers have been together for six years.

MK1 (CHARLIE ~ REAL NAME LOTTE RUNDLE ~ AND SIMEON DIXON)

Fact: MK1's Sim also works as a shoe salesman.

POISONOUS TWINS (STEPHANIE MCMICHAEL AND SOPHIE HOUGHTON)

Fact: The girls are not real twins, but they're great pals.

TIMES RED (STAZ NAIR, SCOTT RITCHIE AND LUKE WHITE)

Fact: The Essex boys have known each other for four years and have been models and waiters, as well as singers.

And of course, our boys: Union J and District 3.

MENTOR: GARY BARLOW (OVER 28S)

BRAD SHACKLETON

Fact: Brad's main hobby is playing polo.

MELANIE MASSON

Fact: The full-time mum-of-two says this was her last shot at working in the industry.

CHRISTOPHER MALONEY

Fact: Christopher's nan inspired him to enter *The X Factor*.

CAROLYNNE POOLE

Fact: Carolynne has a hidden talent – for furniture restoration!

KYE SONES

Fact: A London chimney sweep, Kye sometimes sings to his clients as he works.

NICOLA-MARIE BLOOR

Fact: Nicola used to be a Shania Twain tribute singer.

CHAPTER FIVE

HITTING THE JACKPOT

For GMD3, the trip to Vegas must have felt like a reward for getting through the torture of Bootcamp. Stepping off the plane and into the blazing sunshine they could imagine the fantastic lifestyle they would enjoy... if only they could survive the Judges' House stage.

Checking into their swanky hotel, the boys had little time to relax. Heading for the famous Vegas hotel, Caesar's Palace, they watched in surprise as Louis arrived in a white stretch limo. He told the seven acts: 'I want 100 per cent tomorrow. I want everything tomorrow.'

Joined by a very glamorous-looking Sharon Osbourne, the bands looked overwhelmed by all the glitz and glamour – but excited, too.

'You're in Las Vegas. Superstars from all over the world perform here,' she said, giving them a touch of inspiration.

'You too could have a part of this one day. This is the biggest opportunity you will ever have for your careers – do not waste it!'

The next day would definitely be difficult, but GMD3 were more than ready for it.

Less than twenty-four hours later, the sing-off was underway and each act had begun making their way to have their moment in front of Louis and Sharon.

The boys learned that 'Duke' had already impressed the judges, singing 'The Way You Make Me Feel' by Michael Jackson. Poisonous Twins had performed the Sugababes' 'Freak Like Me' – a song that, if performed right, would be a winner. And happy as they were for the other bands, it must have been hard to muster any enthusiasm to congratulate them because the more impressive they were, the harder it would be for GMD3 to beat them!

This was, after all, a competition. The boys knew they had to put their blossoming friendships aside.

Greg, Mickey and Dan had showcased their boy band credentials flawlessly at their first audition and the trio's electric performance had prompted comparisons with 2010 contestants One Direction. If they had half the success of Harry Styles & co. they would be very happy. And they were fast becoming firm *X Factor* favourites, with their fresh good looks and cheeky personalities.

Of course all that meant nothing if they didn't impress Louis and Sharon. And not all her opinions of the band were positive.

'The pressure from Bootcamp was very hard and difficult, but I believe through that we've got stronger,' said Dan, sitting in the US sunshine with his bandmates while on a rare break from practising.

'We've lived together and that, and we're best mates,' added Greg.

Las Vegas is a definite party town. Everywhere you go, bright lights invite you to go and gamble, dance, eat, drink – most people sleep during the day and stay up all night because the casinos never shut! Under any other circumstances, it would be the perfect holiday for the three young boys, who had long been friends, but not on this trip. In fact, Louis was so worried about the bands partying hard and letting themselves down when they had to sing that he slapped a 10pm curfew on everyone.

The *Sun* reported that he'd given everyone a stern warning, saying: 'Don't let us catch you doing a Prince Harry.' And the contestants were told that 'what happens in Vegas does not stay in Vegas when you're on *The X Factor* – so don't get caught out!'

Speaking at the launch of the show, Louis had admitted earlier that he was toughening up the rules, saying he wouldn't have time for anyone who was hungover while performing. 'I like them to care about the music and be 100 per cent professional,' he told the cameras.

In the back of his mind he might have been thinking about the 2011 contestant Frankie Cocozza, who was booted off the show for his outlandish partying. And after pics of Prince Harry naked and partying in his own Las Vegas hotel had so recently appeared, Louis must have thought he was right to worry. But District 3 were only concerned about impressing their mentor and there would be no late night partying for them.

Not long before they were due to perform, Dermot O'Leary chatted to the boys some more. 'Are you guys confident?' he asked. Mickey took a moment to consider his reply. 'I think we're confident in ourselves,' he said wisely. After all, they had been in a band for a number of years and had worked hard to get their voices working so well together. 'But we're not confident about getting through because there are so many good acts.' And Greg hit the nail on the head totally when he said: 'You don't get an opportunity like this every day.'

Mickey told Dermot that this moment was one they'd wanted for such a long time, before perhaps stating the obvious when he said: 'I think the most important thing about today is to make sure we deliver.'

Ever the professionals, the boys laughed and joked with each other, and to the astonishment of many who were watching them, they even seemed calm and relaxed.

Greg then said: 'Ultimately, we want to prove that we deserve a place in the live shows.'

That evening, they got their chance. It was finally their turn to stand in front of Louis and Sharon and to have their moment. Darkness had fallen and as they waited for Louis to speak, the Las Vegas lights twinkled behind them. Millions of people were starting their nights out – playing roulette, or the slot machines, or even watching mega superstar Céline Dion belt out tunes from the nearby Caesar's Palace Hotel and Casino. None of those tourists had any idea of the nerves eating away at the three special lads, high above them, standing on top of a giant skyscraper.

Louis smiled at the boys to give them a bit more confidence, before asking: 'What are you hoping to get out of today?'

Recalling what he'd told Dermot earlier, Greg said: 'Well today, we really hope to prove to you that we deserve to be in the competition.'

It was a simple statement, but one that was full of heart. Then they began to sing the song that had won them their first boy band battle against Triple J at Bootcamp – 'Bless This Broken Road'.

Louis looked instantly impressed at the quality of the boys' harmonies. As their voices soared and dipped through a range of high and low notes, even Sharon started to smile – and she's a notoriously difficult judge to please!

A moment of silence greeted Greg, Dan and Mickey when they finished singing. It was as if everyone around them needed a moment to take in what they'd just heard – which had been amazing. Then the boys walked off to see Dermot, who was eagerly waiting to hear all about what had happened.

Taking deep breaths, Greg spoke on behalf of the other boys, saying: 'We've done all we can now, so fingers crossed it's enough. I'll not be sleeping tonight.'

Back outside, Louis and Sharon were deep in conversation. Huddling together, Sharon said: 'They're just a delight, aren't they? You can tell they take it seriously.'

It was obvious she had a soft spot for the boys – and who wouldn't! But when Louis asked if there was anything she didn't like about the band, she nodded her head and sighed. 'Yes, the name! It sounds like a virus and doesn't say anything about them.' Those words would have a huge impact on the bandmates' future career, inspiring them to eventually become District 3. But for now, Louis continued to praise the boys – 'I think they're great,' he told her.

Sharon knew he was right but there was one problem that she knew Louis couldn't overlook: it might be hard for the contestants to get up and sing, but it's also extremely difficult for the judges to decide who stays and who goes. After all, they have the hopes and dreams of so many talented singers in their hands. How do they decide who to send on the journey to stardom?

This was exactly what was going through Sharon's head when she said: 'But who do you choose? You're overloaded with boy bands. Which one are you going to pick?'

For Louis it was particularly difficult to decide. While the other judges had six acts to choose from, Louis had seven. He had to keep three and let down four. It was clear that Louis also had a long night ahead of him.

'I don't know,' he admitted sadly.

After a sleepless night for everyone, the boys got dressed and went to see Louis for his verdict. Sitting in the sunshine must have been so pleasant – it was a shame they were feeling so nervous and couldn't just sunbathe by the pool!

Taking a deep breath, Greg said: 'The live shows are literally within touching distance, they're so close. Yesterday we felt like we gave everything we could, today could just change everything for us.'

He put his head in his hands as his friends and bandmates looked on nervously.

'To be able to share this experience together is amazing – it would just be really gutting to see it end,' said Mickey, hoping that wouldn't be the case.

The boys feel silent as they waited for Louis to speak.

'We loved your first audition, your harmonies were amazing and the chemistry between you three boys, and you obviously love your music…' he began.

The boys began to sweat. Usually when Louis started with something positive, it meant there was something bad coming. Just like if he started with an act's bad points, you could usually rely on him ending with good news.

DISTRICT 3

The music industry favourite continued: 'But there are a lot of boy bands out there today. It's a very crowded market and I'm wondering if you bring anything different to the market...'

Dan shut his eyes and nodded his head, looking as if he might cry. Greg put his arm around his two nervous-looking friends, silently telling them it would be okay no matter what Louis said. Even though he knew he'd be equally gutted if they all went home.

'Guys, it's not good news...'

He stopped and watched as Greg, Mickey and Dan hung their heads in defeat.

'It's *great* news! You're through!'

The boys began screaming and jumping up and down. Dan got on his knees and started bowing to Louis, before picking himself up and running off with the others to find Dermot.

'It's the best moment we've ever had, without a doubt,' he told him excitedly.

Dermot was swept away by the power of the boys' emotions. 'It's just going to get better,' he reassured them.

DID YOU KNOW?

Dan Ferrari-Lane is part Italian. His grandfather was called Maud Lane, and his nan was Anna Ferrari. His nan says they're related to the Ferrari car company family. Bet that's revved your engines!

Here are the final thirteen! All these acts made it through to the first live show of *The X Factor* 2012...

James Arthur
Rylan Clark

UNION J AND DISTRICT 3: BATTLE OF THE BANDS

Jahmene Douglas
Jade Ellis
Ella Henderson
Lucy Spraggan
Christopher Maloney (wildcard)
Melanie Masson
Carolynne Poole
Kye Sones
District 3
MK1
Union J

CHAPTER SIX

BECOMING HEROES

WEEK ONE ~ HEROES
6/7 October 2012

What District 3 sang: 'Simply the Best' – Tina Turner

What the judges said:
Tulisa: 'You really made that song your own.'
Gary: 'You've been given the honour tonight of performing first on the *X Factor* live stage.'
Nicole: 'You have such a sweet tone.'
Louis: 'You're simply the best!'

Arriving home from Las Vegas, the boys found it hard to come down from the excitement of the past few weeks. And it probably didn't help that Louis had revealed on television that he thought GMD3 could rival One Direction.

UNION J AND DISTRICT 3: BATTLE OF THE BANDS

Xtra Factor presenter Caroline Flack had asked the judge whether he thought that the three boys were better than Harry Styles & co. and he'd replied: 'From the very first audition I knew they were something special. Vocally, yes – they are world-class.'

Pulling up at the Corinthia Hotel in London, where the boys would be living for the duration of their time on *The X Factor*, they looked very pleased with themselves. Some of the rooms at the swanky hotel cost a whopping £500 a night and the bandmates would have unlimited access to the world-class spa, gym and beauty treatment centre that was on site.

Once they'd checked in, they went up to their rooms, where they found a stand-alone 'rain' shower, deep soaking bathtubs, private bar and even a complimentary newspaper delivery service – well, they would need to find out what was being written about them in all the gossip columns! It was amazing, and unlike anywhere they'd ever stayed before.

Gearing up for their first live performance, they felt a mixture of excitement and nerves. With their adrenaline pumping, the boys began to arrange their vocals to Tina Turner 80s classic, 'Simply The Best'.

But there was something that needed to be done first.

Louis called the boys into his dressing room for a friendly chat, and although Greg, Dan and Mickey knew they wouldn't be getting any bad news, they must have been a bit scared as they knocked on the door and peeped into their mentor's room.

'Hi guys,' Louis said. 'We have a problem.'

The boys stood nervously, waiting for Louis to reveal the reason for their summoning.

'Because you're such a great group, I think you need a great name,' he told them. 'GMD3 isn't right.'

It wasn't exactly a surprise for the trio. Ever since they'd first announced themselves as GMD3 they'd been faced with puzzled expressions everywhere they went. Instantly realising that Louis had a very valid point, their faces lit up with excitement. But how would they decide on their new name?

'I think we should go online,' Louis continued. 'Somebody will come up with an idea for a good name and you can pick the five best for us to choose from.'

The boys nodded in agreement.

Speaking to the cameras later on, they admitted that they had seen it coming. 'When we've introduced ourselves as a band to other people for the first time it's always been "what did you say?" or "sorry?"' said Greg.

And of course Sharon Osbourne had hated the name in Vegas, saying it sounded just like a virus! Besides, name changes were common – Triple J had become Union J and even Louis Walsh had reinvented himself. He was named Michael Vincent when he was born!

'We think it was time for a change,' said Greg, who was fast becoming the spokesman for the group. The boys went on Twitter and asked their fans to send them suggestions. Then they spoke to the national newspapers and appeared on the ITV show, *This Morning*, to make a public appeal.

Presenter Matt Johnson read out some of the ideas, which were coming in thick and fast. 'Ron in Bognor says "Another Direction", Kirsty in Hull says "Which Direction?"…'

Dan informed his hosts that they had three days to come up with a new name, so the pressure was certainly on.

'The original name was the letters of our first names, with a three for the number of us in the group, but people keep thinking we are called GMTV!' the boys grinned. 'It also means we always have to stand in Greg, Mickey and Dan order and we keep forgetting, so that's confusing everyone as well.'

The boys laughed along with the show's hosts before returning to their hotel to go through the submissions – which had begun pouring in.

Sat side by side on the sofa, Greg was in the middle with his laptop perched on his knees. 'Mate,' he said, turning to Dan. 'We've got 1,600 to get through – we've got to be brutal with this!'

Dan looked completely shocked at the number of ideas that had come through. The boys quickly got down to business.

'Greg And His Sausage Rolls', 'Threesome', 'Threeway'… The list went on and on.

'Dead Ferret!' Greg spluttered.

'Oh My Days,' said Mickey, shaking his head.

'Creme Egg?' asked an incredulous Dan.

'Urrrgghh!' they choroused.

Then they came across a few they quite liked – 'Dynamic 3', 'Regeneration', 'Trinity', 'District 3'…

The boys paused. 'District 3?' said Mickey. 'I really like that…'

For three whole days the boys waded through the thousands of submissions, tweeting thanks to everyone who had come up with an idea.

Backstage at the first live show, it was time for the big reveal.

'So,' began Greg, talking to the cameras. 'The public has spoken and the name is…'

Mickey made a trumpet sound and Greg did a drum roll on his leg.

'…District 3!' they choroused, looking extremely pleased. It was a name that very soon the whole country would be talking about.

As well as their name change and the hours spent in rehearsals, the newly named boys had interviews and media appearances to get through, too. It was something they would have to very quickly get used to – all singers and bands have to juggle practising vocals with upping their profiles in the media.

Now magazine took the group to an old warehouse development in the centre of London for an industrial-style photo shoot amid some old factory equipment. The boys were photographed and filmed trying on clothes and posing for the cameras as the photographer asked them to stand this way and that. It was tough work.

When they were interviewed later, Mickey revealed: 'My first kiss was a girl called Ella... Ellie... Ellie,' he said, forgetting the poor girl's name. 'It was under the coats in primary school.'

And Dan scared hundreds of their growing fan base by admitting he fancied fellow contestant Ella Henderson. Greg, meanwhile, said that if he could copy the success of anyone then it would be pop bad boy, Chris Brown.

Mickey said the group aimed to 'take old-school music and make it up to date.' He added that for him, the toughest part of the experience so far had been being away from home. It wasn't all bad, he admitted, saying: 'We get our laundry done for us.'

Lucky boys!

DID YOU KNOW?

Before their trip to Vegas, MK1's Sim broke his ankle playing football, so Charlie had to push him around in a wheelchair the whole time they were in the States. Bless!

UNION J AND DISTRICT 3: BATTLE OF THE BANDS

The boys waited nervously backstage as Dermot O'Leary introduced the first 2012 *X Factor* live show. They were singing first, which was a great honour but also very nerve-wracking. For the audience, there was another surprise in store. All week, fans had been furiously voting for the wildcard act, the one who would fill the coveted thirteenth spot on the show.

Christopher Maloney collapsed in tears when his name was announced. He would be joining James Arthur, Rylan Clark, Jahmene Douglas, Jade Ellis, Ella Henderson, Lucy Spraggan, Melanie Masson, Carolynne Poole, Kye Sones, MK1, Union J and District 3 in the live shows.

Olympic and Paralympic athletes and volunteers were in the audience, and as their new name was called, the stage lights went down and the District 3 boys walked out to a wall of noise. The crowd was going mad before they'd even sung a note!

Wearing hoodies, jeans and trainers, they looked like a proper boy band, illuminated by the dim blue lights. Greg started to sing and Dan and Mickey soon joined in, in their first ever live performance. Lifted up on a platform onstage, the boys squeezed their eyes shut in concentration as they began to sing.

It was a poppy, upbeat version of the original song and they sounded great. Although nervous, they tried their best not to show it and instead as the girls screamed out their names from the audience, they began to enjoy themselves. Their faces were each beamed onto huge screens behind them. It must have been the most exciting moment of their lives.

Louis was visibly proud, smiling and nodding at the boys. And when they finished, it took ages for the cheers to die down before Tulisa could speak.

'Amazing RnB vocals,' she enthused, 'good song choice. You really made that song your own. I haven't heard RnB vocals like that harmonising for a long time. Brilliant!'

The boys hugged each other and looked ecstatic, but it wasn't all good news from the singing star.

'My only criticism would be loosen up and enjoy yourself – less of the boy band faces, just be yourselves and let go.'

The boys took this suggestion on board with a vigorous nodding of their collective heads. They knew they had a long way to go and welcomed the help that knowledgeable Tulisa was giving.

Gary was next. 'Forty-five thousand applications this year – you got through Bootcamp, you got through Judges' Houses and you did a pretty good job,' he said, before his face grew stern. 'I don't know where the talent will spike tonight. I reckon you'll be about in the middle, which means a bit of improvement next week.'

The audience began to boo, so he quickly added: 'But you won't be going home tomorrow night.'

Nicole couldn't wait to give her opinion.

'Boys, if I'm honest,' she said, with a flirty smile, 'you have such a soft spot in my heart.'

The boys looked thrilled to be told these words by such a sexy, older woman. 'Not only are your harmonies on point, you have such a sweet tone, the three of you.'

Blushing, they smiled and thanked her.

Nicole went on: 'I didn't actually love the song choice. I agree with Tulisa – if you're going to go with that song, as soon as the beat kicked in you needed to loosen up and have a bit more fun with it, okay?'

They were wise words from the internationally acclaimed performing artist.

Finally, Louis got to have his say and he was almost bouncing off the walls, he was so excited.

'Guys, I love the arrangement of the song,' he said, revealing that it had been the boys' own idea. 'I love what you do – these boys, you live and you sleep music. You remind me of a young Boyz II Men. You're simply the best!'

Everyone groaned at the joke, and Dermot looked positively pained by it. 'Oh, Louis,' he sighed, standing with the boys on stage. 'We can't start like that, can we?'

'Cheesy!' exclaimed Tulisa from her seat next to the seasoned judge.

Dermot then turned his attention to the boys, whose legs were probably turning to jelly with nerves by now. 'What was it like, opening the show?' he asked, kindly.

'Very scary!' they all agreed.

'It's an absolute honour to open the show with all those millions of people watching,' said Dan.

And millions it was – 9.8 million, to be exact. It was a number that was hard to imagine.

And after that, their first live moment was over. The threesome walked backstage to be greeted by their new friends, the other contestants, who were all nervously waiting their turn to sing.

It had been a thrilling first night. One Direction had surprised them all and turned up to wish everyone luck, before revealing they were backing James Arthur to win.

The 23-year-old followed District 3 on stage, singing a unique interpretation of *X Factor USA* finalist Kelly Clarkson's 'Stronger'.

Fans were transported back to the Sixties when Melanie Masson sang the Beatles' number 'With A Little Help From My Friends', while Lucy Spraggan made *X Factor* history by singing her very own song, 'Mountains'. It was a huge risk but it paid off, and the judges were unanimous in their support of the Sheffield singer.

Having been a wildcard, Christopher Maloney was upset that the judges didn't particularly like his version of Mariah Carey's 'Hero'. Although he had a great voice, Louis joked that he sounded like a cruise ship singer, while Tulisa and Nicole said they thought it was dated.

Fast becoming the party animal of the group, Rylan Clark definitely brought glitz and glamour to the night, with a sparkling performance of Spandau Ballet's 'Gold'. Judge Nicole danced along to his performance, clearly loving every minute of it.

Chimney sweep Kye Sones managed to blow the judges away with his rendition of Michael Jackson's 'Man in the Mirror' – a brave choice. Louis told the 30-year-old: 'That was an incredible performance – you've paid your dues in the music business and now it's your time!'

But if it was Kye's time, what about District 3? It must have been terrifying being backstage that night. Caught in-between feeling happy for their new friends and their own ambition, how on earth could they decide how they were feeling?

The following night, all the acts returned to the *X Factor* studios to hear the results. And much to their relief, the District 3 lads were safe, although they were sad to say goodbye to pretty Carolynne Poole.

Being the first to go must have been awful.

After the live show, the boys spoke to Caroline Flack and Olly Murs on *The Xtra Factor*. Olly and Caroline had presented *The Xtra Factor* together on previous seasons of the show, and now the BFFs had been reunited. Olly – a former

X Factor contestant who has risen to the dizzy heights of international fame – had missed Bootcamp and Judges' Houses that year because he'd been on a huge US tour.

'Look who showed up for work!' joked Caroline, pointing to Olly. 'It's about time, too!'

She then took the opportunity to ask Louis for a divorce! The pair had jokingly got 'married' in Vegas, which is as famous as Gretna Green for impromptu weddings.

'As your wife, I'm entitled to half of everything you own,' she teased, as all the judges erupted into laughter.

Dancer Louie Spence showed the presenting pair how he felt about the girls' performances through the medium of dance, spinning around excitedly, before all the contestants came on to talk about how they thought their first night had gone.

Caroline got her own back on Olly for leaving her alone for the auditions by playing footage from one of his live shows, showing him falling down the stairs in front of thousands of fans.

'That's not funny,' he said, giggling.

'Oh yes it is!' said Caroline, before playing it again.

The duo revealed that all the boys were sharing a suite at their hotel, and that Rylan Clark was making everyone uncomfortable by walking around naked.

'I've sort of put a block on it,' said James Arthur, describing how he was coping with the constant nudity.

Ella Henderson revealed that backstage, the boys spent more time in the make-up chair than the girls. And it was the same at the hotel – the boys were always heading for the spa to get fancy treatments – meaning the girls had to wait in their dressing gowns until they were finished!

It was a fun end to their first week on *The X Factor*.

DID YOU KNOW?

Ella's style icons are Audrey Hepburn and Marilyn Monroe.

CHAPTER SEVEN

LOVE AND COMPETION

WEEK TWO ~ LOVE AND HEARTBREAK
13/14 October 2012

What District 3 sang: 'I Swear' – All4One

What the judges said:
Tulisa: 'You have the strongest harmonies in the competition.'
Nicole: 'I need somebody to rub baby oil all over your bodies!'
Gary: 'I'm very disappointed for you.'
Louis: 'You're a world-class vocal harmony group.'

Greg, Mickey and Dan had mixed feelings going into Week Two of the competition. The boys had loved being on stage, and remembered the rush they'd felt as adrenaline pumped through their bodies like never before; it was truly exhilarating.

They had well and truly beaten Union J, who had been walloped with criticism from the scathing judges, who were disappointed by their performance. But the comments they themselves had received were a bit of a mixed bag, so they knew that they would have to work even harder this week to keep up with the competition.

Ella Henderson and Jade Ellis were getting rave reviews and their voices were amazing. Former shelf-stacker Jahmene had sung such an impressive version of 'Imagine' by John Lennon that the former Beatle's famous lover, Yoko Ono, had tweeted her praise: 'I just saw and heard a recording of @JahmeneDouglas singing Imagine on #XFactorUK – it was beautiful, Jahmene! I love you! Yoko'.

The tweet was seen by millions of people across the globe and propelled him to international fame.

And most importantly, the bandmates could hear Union J practising for Week Two and they knew that they were really going to up their game. There may have been twelve acts left in the show, but really there was only one competition that mattered – between themselves and Union J.

Talent-wise, they were currently very much in the middle of all the acts, and that had to change. It was time to knuckle down to some serious hard work.

Louis sat with them in the rehearsal studios to talk about how they were going to approach Week Two's performance, and to reveal what song he wanted them to sing.

'I've picked a classic ballad for the boys this week,' he had just told the *X Factor* camera crew, 'because these guys can sing anything.'

When Louis told the three boys that they would be singing 'I Swear' – the song made famous the whole world over by nineties boy band, All4One – they were devastated. They had major concerns about singing such an old song and tried to persuade Louis to change his mind.

'Okay, we were meant to be singing "I Swear" this week, but we've thought of two others,' said Mickey, hopefully.

Louis stayed calm and nodded encouragingly.

Given the go ahead, Mickey went on: 'We thought maybe something by Justin Bieber, or "More Than This" by One Direction?'

But Louis's face changed instantly. Suddenly he looked completely horrified.

'How can you do a One Direction song?' he asked, his voice going a little high-pitched. 'Sorry guys, no! Try "I Swear" for me.'

Louis was concerned that the boys, who were very new to the pop world, would be unfavourably compared to the former *X Factor* contestants, who were by now world-famous. In his mind, they simply weren't ready, and it could even damage their fledgling careers.

The boys were nervous. 'It's not… dated, is it?' Greg asked, carefully.

In fact, the song had been a huge hit in 1994, seizing the number one chart spot in several countries, including the US, where it remained for a massive eleven weeks! It had even been certified platinum in the UK and the US, selling 1.6 million copies in the two countries. But Dan was the only band member who was even alive when it had been released, and the boys were terrified that it labelled them as too cheesy in the judges' eyes.

Louis was adamant, so they had no choice but to try their

best with it. So, would the gamble pay off, or would the boys be making a costly mistake?

The boys threw themselves into rehearsals. Over and over, they sang the lyrics, and looked none too happy with how it sounded. They knew that if their hearts weren't in it, the judges would be able to tell, but they couldn't help their reservations: a brand new boy band covering an old boy band's song? This could spell disaster.

That week, the boys practically lived in the rehearsal room. 'Once more, guys,' they told each other, watching themselves in the floor-to-ceiling mirrors that lined the walls. But it was difficult because they weren't keen on the song and finally, tempers started to flare.

'No, no, no! You're doing it all wrong!' Dan yelled at one point, clearly getting frustrated. It was a tense few days as they tried to give the song a fresh sound, one that was all of their own. And having Louis frown at their efforts didn't help either.

Back at the hotel, they sat stony-faced in their suite.

'I'm genuinely worried about this,' Mickey confided to the others, who definitely agreed.

'There's something not clicking with it,' admitted Dan.

But what could they do? Louis was increasingly concerned, too. He was confident that the song choice was good, but he could see the boys didn't like it and he knew that could affect their performance.

Finally, the boys made a decision: they were stuck with the song, so they would be professional about it. They knew it had to be modern, so they concentrated on that. And slowly it began to grow on them.

After a lot of hard work, they had a dress rehearsal on stage to see how it would look to the audience. As they finished, they saw Louis was beaming. 'You've made it your own,' he told them, much to their relief.

After all, Louis had been in the business for years, they told themselves. They would just have to trust him.

DID YOU KNOW?
Jahmene has a strawberry shaped birthmark on his bum!

Meanwhile, according to the newspapers, who were following every move the boys made, things were hotting up back at the Corinthia Hotel. Rumours had been flying that Ella Henderson and George Shelley were dating, after the *Sun* reported that someone had dared them to kiss. But now it seemed that someone else was interested in the pretty 16-year-old – District 3's Dan.

A source told the *Sun*: 'Dan has a crush on Ella – but he can't own up to it now she and George are so joined at the hip.' The newspaper had been told that Ella and Dan had been getting very close in recent days. Was Ella locked in a love triangle with the two boys? If so, this wouldn't be the first *X Factor* romance that viewers had seen blossom before their eyes. During *X Factor* 2011, there were rumours that Frankie Cocozza and Amelia Lily had hooked up, while Rebecca Ferguson and Zayn Malik of One Direction had dated after they appeared on the 2010 series together.

It wasn't hard to see why – all the acts were going through the same experience, living in the same hotel, and spending all their time together. There was bound to be some romance! But both Ella and Dan flatly denied the rumours after reading about them in the national newspapers and magazines.

Ella tweeted: '"Ella and Dan get very close"… REALLY?!!! Why don't we know about this? Hahaaaaa.'

And Dan replied: 'Always the last to know Haha! Thought we were trying to keep it under wraps? LOL… only messin.'

There was no sign of any tension between the lads, however, when one evening the District 3 boys found a learner bike outside their hotel – and decided to jump on it! Along with the Union J boys, they all clambered on it and posed for photos, while their fans laughed along. At one point, Greg had both Mickey and Dan on his shoulders, while sitting on the poor bike. It must have been nice to let their hair down for a few minutes – and their fans loved it, too.

A few days before the lads had also given their fans piggyback rides down the street – aren't they kind?

After intense rehearsals, it was time for them to perform their song, live on *The X Factor*. The quality of the other acts that had gone before them was high, and the three boys were understandably nervous as Dermot announced: 'It's District 3…'

Dan, Greg and Mickey began to sway to the soft music as the cheers from the audience died down to give them a chance to sing.

'I see the questions in your eyes…' Greg began. Was he talking to the judges? Would they question this performance?

It was a soulful rendition of the love song and as the boys sang, vowing never to break hearts, it felt as if they were singing the words directly to each and every girl in Britain. The poignant lyrics continued with a promise to always be there, and the three lads must have thought that they were particularly apt words: 'Stick with us', they seemed to be singing to their fans. 'We'll be there for you if you have faith in us…'

It was a sweet song and the audience seemed to like it but

as they finished, they had to ask themselves the question: Would sweet be enough for the critical judges?

Tulisa's blue eyes looked sincere as she said: 'Guys, I understand why Louis picked that song for you because your strong point is your harmonies, right? And that song is all about harmonies, so it really showed off how good at it you are.'

It wasn't a bad start but the boys could sense there was a 'but' coming.

'I'm going to face the facts here,' she continued, struggling with what she was about to say next. 'When it comes to this competition, you guys are obviously going to be competing with the other boy band in the competition…'

It was nothing they didn't already know – after all, they'd been in competition with Union J since Bootcamp.

'So obviously you've got to up your game and work hard and your strong point, like we saw tonight, is your harmonies.'

Talking about Union J, she said: 'They have a lot of charisma and maybe the strongest individual singers, but you have the strongest harmonies in the competition.'

The boys must have winced when they heard the comparison. Especially since they were getting to know the Union J boys, and were growing to like them. But on this stage it was war and tonight it seemed they were fighting a losing battle.

And it only got worse.

'Tulisa, I couldn't agree more,' said Gary. 'I thought you've had a really bad night tonight – I thought the harmonies were off.'

The audience was baffled. Had they been listening to the same song? Whatever other criticisms the judges made, their harmonies had been beautiful.

'When you watch this back later you're going to be very disappointed,' he told the devastated boys.

Louis tried to spring to their defence, obviously angry with his fellow judge, and asked: 'Are you deaf?'

But Gary went on... *and* on.

'The song choice was very dated, I'm very disappointed for you,' he said matter of factly.

Louis glanced wildly round at the now-booing audience for support and seemed astonished at what he was hearing. But then came the ultimate blow.

'In the Battle of the Boy Bands, I'm afraid Union J have taken it tonight...'

On stage, the boys nodded sadly, defeated by Gary's harsh remarks. And Nicole didn't make things any better either.

Although she agreed with Tulisa that the boys' harmonies were beautiful, she said that they seemed like a slice of warm apple pie – comforting, but not very exciting.

'I wanted you to chuck on some ice cream, shake things up, sprinkle some Tabasco on there,' she told them. 'I need something else from you boys, I need somebody to rub baby oil all over your bodies.'

Even Gary cracked a smile when she said that, and when the audience started to cheer it was obvious that there was no shortage of volunteers!

Maybe the peace-making handshake Gary had given Louis at the start of the show hadn't been quite so sincere as it appeared. The judges had argued about last week's elimination, which Gary blamed on Louis. Was he still angry with him for letting Carolynne Poole go and keeping Rylan?

Was he trying to get back at him by attacking his act?

If so, it was a cruel game of point scoring and very unfair

on District 3. It was up to their mentor, Louis, to comfort the poor boys.

'Boys, that was a faultless performance,' he said, and the boos instantly turned to cheers. 'You're a world-class vocal harmony group, and Gary, I think you're going deaf – I really, really do.'

But the damage was done and standing on stage, the boys must have been thinking that they should have trusted their gut reaction and fought their mentor more on the awkward song choice.

'At first we were a little worried because we didn't want to be just a boy band, doing a boy band song and we didn't want to come across too cheesy,' said Greg.

And hearts all over the country broke when he steeled himself and said: 'Of course we're going to look back over it and any faults we did make this week – if we do get through – we'll make sure won't happen again.'

It was a very professional response, and one that must have been difficult to deliver.

'Alright, boys,' Gary said gently, softening at their honesty.

And with that, the show moved on to the next act.

Greg, Dan and Mickey must have felt awful as they went backstage to try and enjoy the rest of the show but they would have to wait a whole day to find out if singing that particular song had ruined their chance at stardom.

They watched as Jade Ellis sang a soulful and faultless rendition of 'Love is a Losing Game'. She was full of depth and her voice conjured up images of a 1940s starlet in a smoky bar.

James Arthur sang 'No More Drama', winning the judges over with his powerful voice, while MK1 made viewers laugh by trying to teach Louis how to be more 'street' – making him wear a cap, thick-rimmed glasses and oversized headphones. But even as they laughed along, each was a ball of nerves.

After a restless night, it was time to go back to the studio for *The X Factor Results Show*. The contestants were treated to some sensational live performances by Rebecca Ferguson and Taylor Swift, which under any other circumstances the boys would have absolutely adored. But all anyone could think about was that someone would be going home that night…

And after Dermot O'Leary revealed who was safe, District 3 weren't surprised to find themselves in the bottom two, along with the incredible singer Melanie Masson. A sing-off would decide their fate, and they felt they had no chance of competing against such talent.

But there was no time to break down and cry – instead Greg, Dan and Mickey would have to give their last performance of the night everything they had.

'Okay, guys,' said Louis, 'They're gonna sing their hearts out for survival… It's District 3!'

The boys had chosen Bryan Adams' 'Everything I Do' as their 'save me' song. It was a perfect love song, full of heart and longing, and the boys sang it exactly right.

'You can't tell me, it's not worth trying for…'

It was as if they were singing about their own experience, the experience that had led them to that moment on stage, where they were desperately singing to convince the judges to let them continue living their dreams.

Melanie, who has a stunning voice, sang the powerful song 'Stay With Me' and she certainly did it justice. No one knew which way the voting would go.

'That was an amazing, *amazing* sing-off!' said Louis, once both acts had performed. 'Melanie, I love that song; District 3, I love that song.'

Dan Ferrari Lane at GAY in London doing what he loves best: singing.

Greg West has been performing from a young age.
At the *Cosmopolitan* Ultimate Women Awards 2012.

The boys have been performing together since 2010 as GMD3 but changed their name to District 3 during the *X Factor* competition.

Dan and Mickey with their guitars arriving at the studio.

The band enjoys attending fun events as a result of *X Factor*.

Above: At the world film premiere of *Skyfall*.

Below: At BBC's Children in Need, *Shrek the Musical*.

Above and below: District 3 were voted off *X Factor* in week six after going head-to-head with Union J in the bottom two, but it hasn't ended there for the band. Here they're pictured supporting Tulisa at the GAY club in London.

Greg getting into his performance at GAY.

District 3 have a big fan base, but they always make time for their fans.

It was neck and neck – would Louis be loyal to his act?

'I love Melanie an awful lot, but I have to save my own act, District 3,' he added to the boys' relief.

Tulisa looked troubled when it was her turn to speak.

'Melanie, you have one of the most amazing voices in this competition. As for the lads, you have one of the most beautiful harmonies…' she said, undecided. She was struggling to get her words out because she knew someone was about to suffer because of her decision.

'The only thing I can do is go with my heart, and being honest, my heart is with the lads,' she said. 'The act I'm sending home is Melanie.'

Gary gave Melanie another chance by sending District 3 home and setting off another round of boos before it was Nicole's turn to speak.

'First of all, boys, you did an amazing job up there tonight. I know I gave you a hard time yesterday but you showed your true colours today and you knocked it out of the park!'

From behind, a slow chant began, growing louder and louder with each second that passed. 'District 3, District 3, District 3…'

But then she spoke to Melanie, telling her she knew that she had been waiting her whole life for this moment, before saying: 'The act I'm sending home is District 3.'

Deadlock. It would all come down to the public vote.

Dermot O'Leary stood between the two acts, clutching their fate in an envelope. 'The act that received the fewest votes, and the act that will be leaving tonight is…'

He opened it up and read: 'Melanie.'

Backstage, all the contestants began to weep. Melanie had been seen as the mother of the group and was the one everyone went to for a bit of love and advice. Rylan even called her 'Mum'!

After the show, District 3 broke down sobbing, telling Melanie she shouldn't have gone. They felt so guilty that they would go on in the competition while lovely Melanie was going home. The boys would live to sing another day but for the 44-year-old mum-of-two from Glasgow, her *X Factor* journey was over.

Later that night, on *The Xtra Factor*, there was more light relief for the contestants. And another boy band battle took place, this time in the boxing ring for the weekly segment, 'Fighting Talk'.

George from Union J and Dan from District 3 were seen dressed in satin dressing gowns and boxing gloves as they went head to head – verbally, of course.

'You're going down,' said George, getting into the spirit of it.

'No, Shelley's going down,' retorted Dan, as they bounced around the pretend boxing ring.

Question One: How many jobs have you had?

'One,' said Dan.

'Four,' said George.

Round one went to George.

'It was sweeping my dad's coffee factory,' explained Dan.

George listed his work history, which included working in a card shop, two coffee shops and a clothing shop. What a busy bee!

'Yeah, but didn't you get fired from them all?' teased Dan.

'Yeah, but you were sweeping a coffee shop!'

Question Two: What's your shoe size?

'Nine,' said Dan.

'Eight and a half,' said George, admitting defeat.

'You know what they say – small feet, small...' Dan said.

'But you're the only exception, right?' George giggled.

Touché!

Question Three: How many times have you been to the gym this week?

Dan said none, while George said he'd been seven times – the gym bunny!

'Well, you need it,' Dan told him.

'*That* coming from you!' George exclaimed, astonished.

But he didn't need to defend himself in the ring anymore – George had won the fun war of words.

And with that, another boy band battle round went to Union J.

DID YOU KNOW?

Carolynne Poole has acted in ITV soap *Emmerdale* and once toured with Tony Christie.

CHAPTER EIGHT

DAN NEARLY GETS NAKED

WEEK THREE ~ CLUB CLASSICS
20/21 October 2012

What District 3 sang: 'Beggin' – The Four Seasons/'Turn Up The Music' – Chris Brown

What the judges said:
Tulisa: 'Let me tell you something: girls are gonna be attracted to that.'
Gary: 'What a way of coming out of the bottom two last week.'
Nicole: 'You've given the other groups a run for their money.'
Louis: 'We've now not only got one great new boy band, we've got two!'

Greg, Mickey and Dan were understandably low after being in the bottom two the week before, so the first thing Louis did was to sit them down and talk it through.

'Guys, how did it feel? Bottom two on Sunday...'

The boys all looked pained.

'Absolutely terrifying,' said Mickey, sadly.

'Be honest, was it the song?' he asked, carefully. It had, after all, been him who pushed them to sing the Nineties song, something they weren't at all confident about.

'Yeah, I think it was,' said Greg.

But there was no point in wallowing. Instead they talked about what they could do to shine on stage at the weekend.

'I think the thing we're missing in our performance is the energy and the excitement, so this week that's our main focus,' Greg told the *X Factor* cameras.

As they moved between their hotel and the rehearsal studios, they were both pleased and embarrassed to see a gaggle of girls outside their hotel, holding banners and screaming. They felt like rock stars and couldn't resist posing for photos with one or two of them.

And inside the hotel, the boys laughed and joked with each other, putting aside last week's trauma. They were all so close, they were always messing around, touching each other's hair and picking each other up and carrying each other around. Their long friendship made them so at ease with each other, and each of their personalities came out when they were together. It was fun to watch them.

But Louis had noticed something: 'Greg, Mickey and Dan are fun boys, but they've been so focused on the singing that they haven't shown their personalities.'

He had an idea of what would help them prepare for the next live performance and the boys were totally up for it.

Louis was sending them out for the night, to Amelia Lily's birthday bash, so they could enjoy themselves and forget about the competition for a few hours.

And it was a definite success.

Walking through the doors of celebrity club Mahiki, the boys couldn't wait to throw some shapes on the dance floor. After all, this was where Prince Harry went to let loose a little and escape from the pressures of royal life. And if it was good enough for a prince, then it was perfect for the District 3 boys, who deserved some fun. They danced, had a few drinks and mingled with Frankie Cocozza and Kye Sones, but most importantly, they had a real laugh together.

Sometimes you forget who you are when you're so focused on achieving your goals. It always helps to put problems to one side, to be yourself for a little while to get some focus.

'We forgot to let our hair down, basically,' said Greg, the next day. 'Last night we did go out and try to remind ourselves what it is to have fun.'

'Last night was the first time I took my hat off in three weeks,' Dan told the camera, as the boys cheered.

Yuck! Who knows what it was like under there?

Then it was time to go to the dance studio, to work with choreographer Brian Friedman – and some very attractive female dancers! Dan was particularly taken with one of them, pointing to her and giving a cheeky little thumbs-up to the camera. The boys were determined that this week they would enjoy the whole *X Factor* experience so they decided to treat Brian to a few of their own moves.

Prancing around the studio, they did a very good impression of *The Inbetweeners* characters Will, Simon, Jay and Neil when they went on holiday to Malia in the movie. In the film they are in an empty club and try to dance over to some girls but totally embarrass themselves with their awkward moves. Greg, Dan and Mickey got their weird dancing just right, and everyone laughed – apart from Brian.

'It's just an idea,' said Greg, trying hard not to laugh.

'There's no way that's ever happening,' said Brian, sternly.

At this, the boys erupted into fits of giggles like naughty schoolchildren…

The theme of Club Classics was perfect for this new, fun side to the boys and it really lifted their spirits. After one particular rehearsal, Louis was impressed.

'It's fantastic – you are like a new band, there is so much energy!' he told them.

The day before the live show the boys revealed they had decided to ignore Louis' song suggestion that week and choose their own. They told *Tellymix*: 'Louis has been doing this for years and he's got masses of experience but this week, we've chosen our song and it's a lot more energetic than you've seen before. Hopefully, it will go down well. Louis was happy to go with what we wanted to do this week – we don't argue or anything, it's a team.'

The boys seemed a lot happier than they had been at the beginning of the week. It probably helped that One Direction had revealed to *Heatworld* that they were big fans of the new band, describing them as being 'great and talented'!

Harry Styles liked both District 3 and Union J, saying: 'The boy bands are really good. I think it's good that there are two boy bands because a lot of the time I don't really think they want to put two of them through.'

And Louis Tomlinson agreed, saying Union J and District 3 were 'Such nice guys.'

> **DID YOU KNOW?**
>
> Mickey loves roast dinners, especially Yorkshire puddings. Mmm!

The morning of the live show, the boys sat down in front of the cameras to talk about how they were feeling after their week of fun.

'Tonight, we just need to go out there and have fun and just be ourselves,' said Dan.

'Yeah, you only live once,' agreed Mickey.

It was nice to see the boys relax a little. Everyone respected their commitment to their work, but it wasn't healthy to take things so seriously. And they had been badly affected by the sight of poor James Arthur in an ambulance the week before. He'd put so much pressure on himself at the live show that he ended up having a panic attack.

Everyone had been rallying round the singer that week, treating him gently and taking care of him, but it had definitely helped the boys to realise that they just needed to lighten up a little bit. Besides, their fans loved to see them laughing and joking, and happy!

But Louis also made sure they didn't go too wild – unlike Rylan and Lucy Spraggan, who had got so drunk during the week that they'd been thrown out of the Corinthia Hotel.

Lucy tweeted: 'Me and Rylan Clark are partaking in a small vacation from the hotel for a few days. Our most sincere apologies for our behaviour.'

They'd set a very bad example, but not one that the District 3 boys would ever follow. And the hotel must have been much quieter with Rylan gone.

The week flew by and soon it was time to return to the *X*

Factor studio for their third live show. And unbeknownst to the boys, there would be a very special guest in the audience, waiting to see their performance.

DID YOU KNOW?

James Arthur is very untidy – his *X Factor* roommate Rylan Clark says he was constantly tidying up after him.

That week the boys really upped the ante, energy-wise. It was obvious that their fun week had affected them and as they started to sing, the viewers were pleasantly shocked to see that Dan wasn't wearing his usual hat. His hair was as lovely as the rest of him!

Their name was written in huge lights behind them as they sang faultlessly and danced along with the backing dancers. It was a sexy performance and one of the dancers even lifted up Dan's shirt, giving fans a glimpse of his toned chest! The boys loved every minute of their stage time and when they'd finished singing, they heard the biggest cheers they'd had yet and hugged each other with excitement.

'As bad as it sounds, I'm actually happy you were in the bottom two last week because it gave you the kick in the butt you needed to come back fighting and go for it…' began Tulisa.

'The last few performances, you'd sing so sweetly with big smiles on your faces, and you're all good-looking lads,' she added, making the boys blush.

'Let me tell you something: girls are gonna be attracted to that, but what girls are really attracted to is a confidence in here. When you let that out on stage, that's when girls believe it.'

The audience obviously agreed, because once again they began chanting: 'District 3, District 3, District 3…'

Then it was Gary's turn to speak – 'Okay guys, District 3, I have to say, you're the revelation of tonight, you really are.'

Mickey's mouth dropped open in surprise and he hugged his mates as Gary continued.

'What a way of coming out of the bottom two last week, and as Tulisa said, it's been the best thing that's happened to you. Do you know what? I think in the past you've been acting and performing like you think a boy band should perform, but the way you've enjoyed yourself and been yourselves tonight, it's far better – it's more you.'

The boys had shown their true personalities and won themselves a whole legion of new fans in the process. It was turning out to be a great night for Greg, Dan and Mickey.

'You know what?' said Nicole, 'Tulisa's right – it's all about the confidence. We all saw the abs!'

Dan grinned sheepishly.

'And boys, you've given the other groups a run for their money after that. I'm so proud of you guys.'

But it was Louis who reignited the boys' passion to fight for the title of *X Factor* Boy Band of the Year – 'Greg, Mickey and Dan, you worked your arses off all week and like the girls said, getting into the bottom two you knew you had to sing for your lives…'

It was the absolute truth.

'You did it tonight,' Louis went on, 'you sang, you had fun with your performance. We've now not only got one great new boy band, we've got *two* great boy bands in the competition.'

They may have thought they were out of it, but the battle of the bands was back on.

Dermot O'Leary spoke to the lads once the judges had finished their appraisal of the performance. 'You brought the big guns out,' he said. 'How do you feel?'

All the boys were so happy they could hardly speak, but Dan gushed: 'This is the most amazing feeling! You know what? Being in the bottom two, we deserved it last week and it has given us the kick up the **** to do better!'

'When I said bringing out the big guns, obviously these came out as well,' said Dermot, lifting up Dan's shirt to show his impressive abs again.

Every girl in the audience started screaming, making a deafening racket – well, it *was* what everyone wanted to see!

Backstage, the boys were riding high on happiness as they watched all the other acts perform. Jade Ellis had been suffering from a sore throat in the days leading up to her performance and couldn't practise at all. That morning she had tweeted: 'It's killing me not to talk. I've been on voice rest for 48hrs.' But she somehow managed to get on stage and sang her song – 'Free' – beautifully.

Finally the show ended, but before they could go home to bed, there was one more surprise for the lads. One audience member had been very impressed with District 3's performance and felt he just had to go backstage and tell them so: Niall from One Direction!

The bandmates were amazed when he congratulated them and doled out some advice to the boys, who could easily be his future chart competition. And being at the studio had caused memories of his own time on the show to come flooding back. Niall was just sixteen when he was picked to be in One Direction, now an internationally famous band.

'Was incredible to be back at X Factor last night. So strange watching it from the audience,' he tweeted.

And Dan tweeted back: '@NiallOfficial awesome chat with u tonight mate! Hopefully see u soon :D'.

It had been an amazing night for the boys but as always, you never knew what was going to happen on the results show. They just had to cross their fingers and hope they'd go through.

The next night, District 3 stood on stage with all the other acts to sing 'Ain't Nobody' by Rufus and Chaka Khan. It was a great way to kick off the show, but until they heard the results no one could truly relax.

'In no particular order, the first act returning is Union J,' announced Dermot O'Leary.

Greg, Dan and Mickey watched as their boy band rivals celebrated, waiting to hear their own name.

Dermot read out more names: Ella, James Arthur, Rylan, Christopher Maloney, Jahmene... There was only one more name to call – would the boys be in the bottom two again? After all their hard work, could they really be going home?

'...and District 3!'

The bandmates were so happy they threw their arms around Louis, then each other before Dan jumped up on Mickey's shoulders. Then as he got off, they hugged all of Union J, too.

MK1 and Kye were in the sing-off and after it went to a deadlock it was revealed that MK1 had received the fewest votes. It was time for them to go home.

The next day Charlie and Sim spoke to the *Daily Mirror* about their defeat. While they had taken it graciously on the show the night before, they were upset now, and had a little moan about the judges – who they claimed had talked throughout their performance.

And they even had a few choice words to say about Christopher Maloney.

'Chris surviving was a bit of a shocker,' said Sim. 'He is the biggest diva.'

Now, now, guys...

> **DID YOU KNOW?**
> Lucy Spraggan's *X Factor* audition has been seen over 11 million times on YouTube!

CHAPTER NINE

TAKING A STEP BACK

WEEK FOUR ~ HALLOWEEN
27/28 October 2012

What District 3 sang: 'Every Breath You Take' – Sting/'Beautiful Monster' – Ne-Yo

What the judges said:
Tulisa: 'I felt like you dropped it a little bit in your vocals.'
Nicole: 'You're scaring me right now!'
Gary: 'This week was a massive step back.'
Louis: 'Guys, okay, it wasn't as good as last week.'

The boys were giggling in their hotel room as their outfits were laid out on the bed. It was Halloween and Rylan's birthday, and there was going to be a huge party. It was a chance to let their hair down again and the boys couldn't wait. They were going to exclusive celebrity club Mahiki, again.

Tulisa and Nicole were going, too and it was going to be awesome. Girls always wore skimpy outfits at Halloween and they couldn't wait to see what the bombshells would be wearing! Dressed as little devils, they took a cab to the club and got ready to have a top night.

Rylan was over the top as always, dressed as a dead American Footballer, and was prancing around, having fun. But as the boys looked around, they wondered where Nicole was.

Tulisa was chatting to the other contestants in a very sexy Dracula outfit. She had fake blood pouring down her neck and was wearing vampire teeth. She looked amazing!

But while everyone else was there, Nicole was nowhere to be seen. Then a huge cake was wheeled in and everyone was shocked when she burst out singing 'Happy Birthday', in true Marilyn Monroe style.

Wearing a red leather basque and fishnets, she went over to sit on Rylan's lap as everyone whooped and cheered. Jaws were definitely hitting the floor all over the club, especially when she and Tulisa posed together for photos. There was plenty of free drink and Greg, Dan and Mickey enjoyed letting off steam. They had been working so hard, it was nice to finally relax. And the whole night must have felt like a dream – they were partying with a Pussycat Doll and one third of N-Dubz!

They didn't get back to the hotel till 4am – and when they did, they found Christopher Maloney literally sprawled out on the floor!

The next day, Greg told the website *DigitalSpy*: 'We tried to get him into bed and that, but he was literally completely passed out. We were like, "Come on, Chris, go to bed mate, you've got to get up for rehearsals," but he was having none of it.'

The trio said they had given Chris a little bit of a tormenting, even slapping him lightly now and again to try and get him up. But they had to admit they had occasionally enjoyed a drunken night out themselves. When asked which member of the band was the worst drunk, they settled on Mickey. Apparently he changes completely and likes to get naked on a night out.

'I've got far too many pictures of Mickey when he's just fallen asleep on top of his bed, naked,' said Greg.

It had been a late night and everyone had to be up at 8am for rehearsals. But the boys deserved it and they loved dancing and chatting, and drinking with everyone.

Dan made a new friend that week, too – in former glamour model Katie Price. Katie, who was mates with Rylan, had come to see him at the hotel and booked a room for the night. Dan was invited along and all three sat and watched a movie in her room. How surreal!

Dan later told *Heat* magazine: 'She came to the hotel to see Rylan and she asked to meet me and the rest of the band. We went to her room and just chilled for a few hours. That's how we first met.

'Rylan told me she fancied me and I thought, "Oh no, no way! Why would she fancy me?"'

Dan was baffled by the attention, but he wasn't going to turn it down, as he confessed: 'I was very shocked but I fancy her myself. I've always been a massive Katie Price fan. I'm a fan of her boobs! They're massive!'

He told the celebrity magazine that Katie had been

texting him, too. But if she did fancy Dan, she wasn't going to let on about it. And her spokesperson totally denied that there was anything romantic going on between them, as did Rylan.

'Basically, I gave Kate Dan's number,' he revealed to the *Sun*. 'And they just had a couple of texts, nothing happened, harmless flirting, whatever – Kate's a single girl, Dan's a single guy, good luck to them all.'

But a few weeks later, Kate's ex-boyfriend, Leandro Penna, said something very different. He told *Reveal* magazine: 'I finally decided it was the end when she messaged Dan Ferrari-Lane from *The X Factor*'s District 3. I'm sure she has no interest in him and did it to get in the media, and I don't agree with that. I felt so betrayed, I could no longer forgive her.'

Poor Dan! He also revealed that he was single and didn't want a relationship before *The X Factor* show was over. 'I'm here to concentrate on the music and then I can have some fun with all the girls afterwards,' he said.

Girls everywhere must have been devastated. Be patient, ladies!

'I do have a bit of a type,' he continued. 'I like older women, but I'm not sure if all the older women over thirty are into me.'

Don't worry, Dan – we think you'll have plenty of women to choose from!

During the week, the guys came up with a cunning plan. The competition was definitely hotting up now so they decided to spy on Union J to see how their rehearsals were going.

As Josh, Jaymi, George and JJ went over their song the

cheeky District 3 boys grabbed walkie-talkies and crept up to listen at their hotel door.

But they were spotted…

'This is not on!' Jaymi told them, pretending to be serious as Greg, Dan and Mickey ran away, laughing.

Then Jaymi turned to the others and said: 'This means war!'

Later that day, District 3 were exercising in the hotel's gym when the Union J boys crept up behind them and found the plugs for the treadmill.

'Do it now!' Josh told George, who flicked the switch, giggling.

All the equipment turned off, and the treadmills ground to a halt.

'What's going on?' said Greg, before he spotted the Union J boys legging it for the door.

The things those lads got up to in their hotel!

The day before the live show, the boys gave an extremely revealing interview to *DigitalSpy* – and not all of it was very endearing.

Greg and Dan both joked that Mickey's vocal warm ups, which he performed while preparing to sing, sounded like a police siren.

'Mickey's vocal warm-ups,' said Greg, 'they are the most annoying. It's just the sound he makes – I don't know how it warms him up.'

Mickey tried to defend himself from the embarrassing accusation, saying: 'I don't do that,' but Greg cut in: 'It's a siren, basically. It's got a real rasp to it.'

'Dan's been wearing the same pair of socks for the last four days,' Mickey shot back. 'What I find annoying is that they walk around with bare feet and with athlete's foot, that's annoying.'

'Outrageous!' chorused the others.

The *DigitalSpy* readers then got to work, tweeting the boys some very bizarre questions, and as a result they got some equally bizarre answers!

All of them said they would prefer not be able to sing, if it meant they could carry on eating McDonald's. And when asked who was the smelliest, Dan said that the 'rising' smell of Greg's feet was a big problem.

'When we used to all live in the flat in Windsor, I had the bunk bed on the top and heat rises,' he recalled. 'I was down one end and he was at the opposite, and it would rise up and it was not nice.'

Asked whether they would rather eat the fluff from a tramp's bellybutton or go without sex for a year, Greg joked 'both' before they all agreed that they would choose the belly button fluff. Nice!

Dan decided he would rather be dumb and beautiful while the other two said 'smart and ugly', prompting Greg to joke that Dan was definitely the vain one. All jokes aside, the boys were their typically humble selves, with Dan saying that out of all the acts, District 3 did not deserve to win despite all the hard work that they had been putting in.

Finally, when asked out of all the acts which they would like to see win other than themselves, the group picked James Arthur.

Earlier in the week the boys had the chance to dust off their best clobber when they rubbed shoulders with Hollywood royalty at the James Bond premiere of *Skyfall*. Photographers shouted to get their attention as they arrived together, all dressed like James Bond himself.

Greg wore a two-piece navy suit, with black lapels and a

navy and white spotted bow tie. He looked so cute! Dan donned a traditional suit in dark blue, with blue lapels, while Mickey went for a three-piece, with the jacket and bow tie in blue, and the trousers in black. They all looked really swanky.

All three were later pictured larking around with the other finalists in the programme, obviously enjoying such an exciting occasion. And they had even more fun in the make-up studio two days later, when *X Factor*'s chief make-up artist, Julia Carta, gave them a Halloween make-up challenge to perform.

'You've got two minutes to make Dan look as gruesome and gory as possible,' she told Greg and Mickey, who instantly began to chuckle. This was going to be fun!

The boys sprang into action and covered his face in whatever they could get their hands on. 'Try not to get it in my eyes,' said Dan, squinting as the other boys dolloped huge amounts of black greasepaint onto his face.

'And you've got to give me a monobrow!' he ordered.

'I don't know what that is,' said Mickey, picking up the various sparkly pots and cases.

'Dan, you've got a fantastic jawline, mate,' said Greg, as he painted yet more black stuff on his friend's face.

About halfway through, Julia looked puzzled – Dan just looked a mess! 'What look are you going for, guys?' she asked.

'A sort of a Jekyll and Hyde look,' Greg said, confidently.

With waterproof gel eyeliner, Mickey gave Dan the monobrow he had asked for. Bet that took a while to get off! And they even gave him a luscious red pout with some lippy.

'Not in my mouth!' said Greg, spitting it out.

All three boys dissolved into fits of giggles when Mickey reached for something purple to cover Dan's nose in. They had ten seconds left – this was ridiculous fun!

In the end, Dan looked pretty horrifying – and even Julia was quite impressed.

'It's the latest look, innit?' joked Mickey.

But Dan just shook his head and said: 'Look what they've done to me!'

After cleaning up, the boys also got to meet a mega, mega star – Robbie Williams. He had dropped by to give all of the contestants some advice and the threesome listened carefully to everything he had to say. Robbie is a master performer and the boys wanted to know everything they could about entertaining the crowds.

Then it was time to show off that new knowledge, in their fourth live performance on the *X Factor* stage.

DID YOU KNOW?

Jahmene Douglas regularly sings with the gospel choir at his local church.

Appearing as silhouettes against a creepy street scene, when the spotlights hit the boys, everyone could see they were dressed in more Halloween costumes – this time as the scary killers from Stanley Kubrick's *Clockwork Orange* film. Twirling canes, they sang softly to 'Every Breath You Take', before the music changed and suddenly they were leaping about to Ne-Yo's 'Monster'.

Dancing between fake gravestones the energy was amazing and their dance moves were faultless but their voices wavered a little as they got out of breath from bouncing around. They really got the crowd going, though and when they finished everyone cheered. But the judges weren't so keen.

'Guys, I absolutely loved it when you started off,' Tulisa began. 'When you dropped off into Ne-Yo, because of all the dance moves it felt like you dropped it a little in your vocals, which is a surprise for you guys.'

It was a disappointing start, but Tulisa was sweet when she finished off by saying: 'All in all, I thought it was a good performance. I did love the energy and the moving about.'

Gary wasn't so kind, though. 'I felt like last week was a massive step forward – this week was a massive step back,' he said, before describing the performance as 'an absolute musical mess'. 'Your vocals weren't strong this week either. I'm so disappointed for you guys, I really thought you were coming back fighting.'

The boys were obviously sad but tried to keep their spirits up, helped by one girl in the audience who screamed: 'We love you!' as loud as she could.

Nicole, meanwhile, looked pained. 'I love the song you started out with. It was so beautiful, so rich,' she said. 'Monster obviously is in the wrong key for you guys, which you can't change because it's a mash-up. I don't like the mash-up this week.'

She also said that the boys' eye make-up was scary – they had tiny eyes painted on their faces, giving them each five eyeballs. Urgh!

And there was no back up from their mentor, either. The boys were shocked to hear Louis agree with the other judges, saying: 'Okay, it wasn't as good as last week, but you can sing, you can dance and you bring energy to the show, so guys, give them a chance.'

On stage, the mood was low, but Dan saved the day with

his cheerfulness. 'We appreciate your comments,' he told the judges. 'We're trying to find the right balance in terms of what we're gonna do, but with the mash-up – it's Halloween and it's the monster mash-up!' he said, shrugging his shoulders and smiling.

Mickey and Greg started cheering along with the audience, impressed at their bandmate's strength. It hadn't been a good night and who knows how badly they must have slept, but the following evening they were shocked to discover that despite the judges' comments, they were safe. Instead their rivals, Union J, had the horrible experience of singing against the phenomenal Jade Ellis.

After JJ, Josh, George and Jaymi were saved by the judges, Jade sadly went home. The Battle of the Bands would rage on for at least one more week.

That night on *The Xtra Factor*, Caroline Flack handed Rylan a very special birthday card. When he opened it up, he was shocked to see it was from his nemesis, Gary Barlow!

'Oh, he's spelt my name wrong!' the Essex boy laughed – he'd found a rogue 'd' at the end of Rylan. But maybe the beautifully wrapped present that came with it would make up for the mistake.

Rylan burst into fits of giggles as soon as he saw what it was – a book called *Singing for Dummies*!

James Arthur was teased mercilessly about taking several girls back to his room after the Week Three results show and he revealed that they had all stayed overnight.

And Caroline said she'd discovered that District 3 had retweeted comments about themselves on Twitter a massive 2,012 times – it's a wonder they managed any rehearsing at all!

DID YOU KNOW?

Mickey still doesn't know the difference between a mongoose and a meerkat!

CHAPTER TEN

NICOLE SHEDS
A TEAR

WEEK FIVE ~ NUMBER ONES
3/4 November 2012

What District 3 sang: 'Dynamite' – Taio Cruz

What the judges said:
Tulisa: 'You've overstepped the cheese mark…'
Gary: 'They can do better than that.'
Louis: 'You know they can sing.'
Nicole: 'This is *X Factor*, where they eat you alive.'

The bandmates were feeling very reflective when they woke up on Monday morning. It had just started to sink in that they were in *The X Factor*, a competition that could really launch their careers.

UNION J AND DISTRICT 3: BATTLE OF THE BANDS

And now the boys, who had known each other since their school days, were all in it together. They were staying in an amazing hotel, spending their time with singing coaches and choreographers – and basically doing the things that they used to fantasise about with each other.

'Doing this competition with your best mates is just incredible,' Mickey decided to reveal to the *X Factor* cameras. 'We decided two years ago, let's make a band.'

Greg added: 'And the next day we just rehearsed a song. It was "Crawl" by Chris Brown.'

The video is still on YouTube, and the boys look very sweet as they sing the song, but they've obviously come a long way since then.

'It wasn't one of our best,' Greg has since admitted.

Louis took some time to speak to them about what makes a good boy or girl band. 'Guys,' he said, sitting with them in the rehearsal studio. 'I've worked with bands like Boyzone, Westlife, Girls Aloud – and it takes them a long time to get to know each other and get natural chemistry, but you have that already.'

It was one of the things that definitely made them stand out – apart from their 'schamazing' voices and gorgeous faces, of course. Everyone had praised them for their vocal harmonies, saying they were way better than Union J's. But that kind of unity comes with practice, and the District 3 boys knew each other's voices perfectly. They hoped it would give them the edge over the other band who were already doing very well in the competition.

Later on, Greg, Mickey and Dan got to meet No Doubt and were totally starstruck. When lead singer Gwen Stefani said 'hi', none of them knew what to do. 'Oh wow, hi, you alright?' said Greg, eventually leaning in for a cheeky kiss.

The famous rock band asked the boys if they felt less nervous as the weeks had passed, and they were quick to say: 'No!'

'It's difficult 'cause recently we've been doing all choreography stuff as well and that's not really what we're used to,' admitted Greg.

'I'm not good at choreography, either,' said Gwen, putting the boys at ease. If mega stars like Gwen Stefani still struggled, then they weren't alone.

The boys had a lot of moves to practise and spent a lot of time with the pretty dancers who would be on stage with them on Saturday. Dan was chuffed to get a hug from one of them and couldn't believe his luck. Greg fanned himself with his shirt – it was getting steamy in the studio!

Mickey was worried that the rehearsals could be awkward because they didn't think they were very good with girls. He decided to show Greg his best chat-up line, saying: 'Touch this,' while pointing to his hoodie. Greg had a squeeze, but groaned when Mickey said: 'Does this feel like boyfriend material to you?'

Worst chat-up line, ever!

But his lines were obviously working for the cheeky chappie because the *Sun* revealed that he'd managed to pull *two* girls in the hotel bar that week. After chatting to two very sexy ladies from millionaires' playground Monaco, they were soon buying him drinks!

A source told the paper: 'Mickey made a beeline for the girls as soon as he clapped eyes on them. They were eighteen, just like him, and the three of them had plenty in common.' After a bit of banter, Mickey apparently disappeared with the girls – and was later seen snogging one of them in the five-star hotel's atrium. Lucky girl!

The other boys weren't missing out in the love department, either. Greg told the *Sun* that one female fan had been leaving some very odd love tokens at the hotel.

'There's a girl who has been sending us stones – love heart stones,' he said. 'We've now got more than ten stones, but don't know what to do with them all!'

But while they had been charming their female fans, relations with Union J were rumoured to be getting frosty. So far the groups had each had to sing once for survival and there would only be one winner of *The X Factor* so it was only natural that they would compete.

Someone from the show revealed to the *Sun*: 'There is clearly tension between the two bands. Both are rehearsing like crazy and making sure they always go and see their fans. They hardly speak to each other any more.'

Could this be true?

Two days before the live show, both District 3 and Union J received a boost from fellow boy band and previous *X Factor* favourites, JLS. The quartet of Aston, Oritsé, J.B. and Marvin said they were fans of both groups – but issued a warning for them if they wanted to continue being popular.

Aston told *DigitalSpy*: 'Those two boy bands are going to have to come out with something extremely different from what's in the market now. You've got the likes of us, The Wanted, 1D, Lawson. You've got a total mix and it's going to be hard to find your own lane.'

DID YOU KNOW?

If Kye Sones could meet anyone in the world it would have to be HM the Queen. What a patriot!

As the boys were announced on the live show that Saturday,

they surprised everyone by appearing through the audience instead of on stage. There were lots of bright lights and dancers – their performance of Taio Cruz's 'Dynamite' was very energetic. But with all the bouncing around, their vocals suffered.

And the judges weren't kind at all.

'Oh guys,' said Tulisa, shaking her head. 'Guys, oh, I love you, guys! This is gonna pain me to say this: Louis, you've got it wrong this week.'

The audience booed and Louis stepped in, saying: 'No, no way!'

'You've overstepped the cheese mark,' she added. 'It felt so awkward for me. I could see, bless your little souls, you're thinking of the choreography and you're trying to sing at the same time.'

The boys looked very upset. It had been such a struggle for them to learn all their moves and they'd worked so hard. But Tulisa wasn't blaming them – it was Louis who had given them too much to think about that week, she said. Learning a song and an energetic dance routine in just six days is very difficult.

'I keep thinking back to when we first saw you guys,' said Gary. 'You were a vocal harmony band – very technical, very good singers – somewhere that has got completely lost.'

Greg put his hand to his head, trying to shield his embarrassment from the audience. The acts all feel very exposed up there, especially when things aren't going well. It was like being told off by the headteacher in front of the whole school – not nice at all.

'I don't know how else to say it, but no, baby, no!' Nicole said, wagging her finger.

'Yes baby, *yes*!' said the ever-loyal Louis.

Nicole told him: 'Louis, you got it wrong with the song – they're great with their harmonies.'

The crowd felt for the boys. They started chanting again: 'District 3, District 3, District 3…'

Greg, Dan and Mickey slowly began to smile. It was great to know the audience was behind them.

Nicole had to shout over the noise to continue. 'If we were at *The Mickey Mouse Club*, this would be schamazing,' she said, referring to the American show, where Britney, Christina Aguilera and Justin Timberlake were made stars. 'But this is *X Factor*, where they eat you alive! It's not fair – you can't have the boys come out there and do that, and then you have Union J do what they do.'

It was so harsh – the last thing they wanted to happen was to be compared to their biggest rivals on the show. Inside, they must have been cringing.

'They can do better than that,' interrupted Gary, defending the poor lads.

And when Louis got his chance to speak, he was on their side, too. 'But guys, you know they can sing,' he told his fellow judges. 'Listen, I thought it was fantastic. I think the people at home are gonna vote for you guys.'

And when they heard the resounding cheers from the audience, Greg, Dan and Mickey started to believe it. But they were still upset.

DID YOU KNOW?

District 3 fans are called '3eeks' and Union J fans are known as 'J Cats'.

On *The Xtra Factor* that night, Louis said he was very concerned about District 3. 'I'm worried after the savaging from the judges,' he told Tulisa, Gary and Nicole. 'It was uncalled for, guys.'

But the other judges stuck by what they had said. 'It was a cool song, man, and you made it uncool,' said Nicole, blaming Louis for their bad performance.

Dermot O'Leary asked her who she thought would be leaving and she said: 'Unfortunately, based on tonight, I think it will be District 3.'

And Gary obviously thought the same, because he said: 'Those guys are really good singers and I felt sorry for them tonight – it felt like a pantomime on stage.'

Olly Murs and Caroline Flack spoke to Greg, Dan and Mickey, asking: 'How are you feeling?'

Mickey was the first to answer. 'Yeah, we're alright – a little bit deflated – but we're gonna try and keep our heads up and stay strong.'

Caroline then asked if the boys thought the criticism was too harsh and Greg replied: 'I agree with it to some extent. We've got to this stage of the competition, we've done the first few weeks of the "lives" and it is what we like to do, but maybe it isn't enough. We've really tried to up the stakes and energy.'

Most of the guests on the show were convinced that District 3 would be leaving the next day, which can't have been very nice to hear.

Olympic medalist Greg Rutherford, presenter Amanda Byram and DJ Scott Mills all said they thought it was the end of the road for the group.

It wasn't sounding too good for the boys but at least they had support from One Direction's Niall Horan, who tweeted: 'Great job lads! I'll be voting! Fingers crossed boys!'

And Taio Cruz, whose song they had sung, also tweeted

his support. Their hoards of fans were kept busy all night, trying to drum up votes for the band – but would this be enough?

The next night, worried and a bit scared, the boys went back to the studio for *The X Factor Results Show*.

Rita Ora sang 'Shine Ya Light', and No Doubt sang 'Looking Hot', providing an amazing distraction for Greg, Dan and Mickey, who must have been convinced they would be in the bottom two.

But in a shocking turn of events, when Dermot O'Leary read out the list of acts that would be going through to Week Six, District 3 was one of them! Clearly relieved, the boys nearly collapsed – they hadn't been expecting this at all. Instead Kye Sones and Rylan Clark battled it out in the bottom two, with Rylan emerging victorious.

It was a close call for the boys – things were getting very serious. But as usual, on *The Xtra Factor* there was light relief for everyone. It was time for another bout in the pretend boxing ring.

'Tonight, on Fighting Talk – Josh from Union J vs Greg from District 3!' boomed the announcer. Their nicknames were 'Baby Face' and 'The Virus'!

'I'm going to knock you into another history,' pretended Josh, who was wearing red.

'What's that?' asked Greg, pointing behind him and making him look – but there was nothing there. He's such a funny guy!

Question One: How many bones have you broken?

'Seven,' said Josh.

Greg looked shocked. 'Really?' he said, looking concerned for a moment. 'How'd you manage that? I've broken no bones.'

'I've broken this wrist three times,' he said, pointing to his right, 'my left wrist once, I've chopped off a thumb…'

Yikes!

Round one went to Josh.

Question Two: How many piercings do you have?

'Two,' said Josh. Meanwhile, Greg shook his head in defeat as he mumbled: 'One.'

The two boys discussed piercings for a moment. 'I was thinking of getting a Prince Albert, but bottled it,' Greg revealed. Ouch!

Question Three: How many teeth have you had removed?

'Two,' said Josh.

'Three,' said Greg, going in for a pretend punch.

Round three went to Greg!

'I haven't had them taken out by a dentist – I had them out by a football boot,' explained Josh. Broken bones, missing teeth – how on earth does he still look so pretty?

Greg was shocked, too. 'You're *joking*!' he said. 'Let's have a look…'

'Winner, winner, chicken dinner!' chanted Josh, before pretending to knock his rival out.

Greg did a very convincing collapse – you could tell he has had stage training!

That night before they went to bed, the boys had time for one more tweet. 'Just wanna say thankyou to all u incredible people who have voted for us!! Appreciate u all soooo much and will repay the favour one day!'

DID YOU KNOW?

Dan puts honey in his tea to give it that extra bit of flavour. He also loves Greg's mum's spag bol.

CHAPTER ELEVEN

THE DREAM
IS OVER

WEEK SIX ~ BEST OF BRITISH
10/11 November 2012

What District 3 sang: 'Tears In Heaven' – Eric Clapton

What the judges said:
Louis: 'You're a brilliant vocal harmony group.'
Nicole: 'You just brought tears to my eyes!'
Tulisa: 'My favourite performance yet.'
Gary: 'Great to see you back where you were when we chose you to be in the finals.'

The boys woke up on Monday morning feeling very confused. They'd had two weeks of bad comments from the judges and it was very draining, feeling so anxious all the time. Plus, they didn't quite know how to please the judges anymore. First they'd said they wanted more energy from the boys, then they said they preferred it when they had stuck to what they knew – amazing vocal harmonies. There was no pleasing them lately. But they wanted to pay attention to the judges so they decided to strip everything back and concentrate on showing off their beautiful voices.

'I'm actually so happy Gary said he feels like he doesn't know who we are anymore,' Dan told the *X Factor* cameras. 'It's given us the opportunity to go back and do that.'

'Knowing that we're halfway through the competition makes us even more hungry for it,' said Greg. 'And the support we've been getting has been absolutely amazing. We really don't want that to end.'

It felt like every single day they'd been signing autographs and having their picture taken. And they loved every minute of it.

Louis sat them down to decide on that week's song choice.

'Right, guys – it's the Best of British! We've got an amazing catalogue of songs,' he told them, enthusiastically.

And the boys agreed.

'From the Beatles to the Stones to Coldplay… I want your input,' he added.

They had a brainstorming session. There are so many great British songs to choose from, it must have been a tough decision!

'We were thinking maybe "Freedom"? What do you think to that?' asked Dan.

'George Michael? We can do better than that,' replied Louis. 'It's a bit karaoke.'

'An RnB version of "Can't Buy Me Love"?' suggested Mickey.

'How does that go?' asked Louis, showing his age.

The boys instantly sang a version and it sounded great. But it was just one choice of thousands.

Louis later said: 'It was really tough because we all had different ideas for songs. We tried the Beatles, we tried Sean Jay, we tried Phil Collins, but eventually we decided on Eric Clapton – "Tears in Heaven".'

It was a beautiful choice – a melancholy ballad, perfect for the boys' voices. Clearly happy with the decision, they stripped everything back, cut out all the choreography and dancers, and focused rehearsals on their vocals.

'So excited for this weekend,' they eventually tweeted. 'Going back to our old style of music! Harmonies!!'

After rehearsals on Monday night, the boys were photographed looking confident, with Mickey even seen carrying a huge keyboard out of the rehearsal studio under his arm.

As fans ran up to score autographs and kisses from their idols, Dan and Greg laughed and joked with their admirers and photographers acting as security guards did their best to prevent things from getting out of hand.

On the Friday, the boys really wanted to go downstairs and see the fans who were gathered outside but their security wouldn't let them.

They tweeted: 'For the girls outside the Corinthia hotel…x We're not allowed out because security says you've been fighting and it's too dangerous?'

No one wants to get in the middle of girls who are scrapping, so the boys stayed in until the kerfuffle had died down.

The night before, Mickey Parsons had been feeling a bit under the weather so he stayed in while the rest of the

District 3 boys went out to celebrate the launch of the Kardashians' new fashion collection in London.

Proudly sporting their Remembrance Day poppies, Greg and Dan posed with Jahmene for pictures, making it look as if they'd swapped Mickey for the soulful singer. And they took full advantage of his absence, telling journalists that he was definitely the biggest backstage flirt.

'He's told us he's ill, but we don't believe him – he could just be flirting with someone,' they joked.

But the tables were turned when one journalist spotted a bright red kiss mark on Dan's cheek and teased him about it.

'One of the fans outside the hotel kissed me – I didn't realise she was wearing lipstick,' he explained, blushing, as Greg kindly wiped it off for him. Aw!

Polite Mickey did the right thing and apologised to Kim Kardashian for his absence at the fancy do, tweeting from his sickbed: 'Sorry I couldn't be at your Kollection launch tonight – a bit poorly, lying in bed, but hope you had a great night xxx'.

The guys had rehearsed relentlessly all week and when they woke up on the day of the sixth live show, they were feeling excited. 'Such a big day ahead,' they tweeted. 'Early morning feeling but excitement starting to kick in.'

They were ready to rock!

The boys hopped into the bath to get ready for the day – and then decided to recorded themselves in there for their fans! Viewers saw Greg in the hotel bath, covered in soapsuds as he thanked everyone for their support.

'We've actually got a very special guest with us today,' he said, cheekily. 'Here to join us is the one and only Mickey P…'

And as if from nowhere, up popped Mickey, his head

covered in bubbles. He'd been hiding behind Greg in the bathtub. Oo-er!

'Hello, guys,' he said. 'We're together...'

'Yeah, we scrub together,' said Greg. 'D's already been in, he's just drying off now. Anytime you want to come join in the tub, just let us know.'

It would have to be a *very* big bathtub to fit all the District 3 fans in!

The short movie ended with Mickey and Greg snuggling up together in the tiny bath – and it was an instant hit with the fans. It's been seen by over 28,000 people on YouTube since they posted it!

When they were dry, the boys enjoyed some fabby District 3 cupcakes that a fan had made for them. They looked amazing, all decorated in icing, saying: 'Good Luck District 3'. How sweet is that?

To pass the time until their big performance, the boys played a game of 'guess who' online with their fans, posting some famous British song lyrics for their 3eeks to guess. It was a nice way to try and relieve the stress they must have been feeling about that night's show.

Celeb website *sugarscape.com* released their 'Hottest Lad Of The Year 2012' shortlist, and the three boys were excited to see they were all there, alongside all the One Direction boys, Hollywood star Channing Tatum and even *Vampire Diaries* hottie, Ian Somerhalder.

Bet that cheered them up!

And the bandmates were overjoyed when the 33 Engineer Regiment turned up to show their support. 'We salute you!' they tweeted. 'Amazing people!'

It had been a busy day, they reflected, as they were driven to the studio. And despite their nerves, the boys were excited about the live show that night. It must have felt strange, being so excited and so nervous at the same time.

Louis told them: 'Tonight is your big chance. I know the song's great, I know you can sing it – so go out and kill it!'

Just before they went on stage, they boys tweeted: 'We're getting ready!! See you in a second 3eeks.'

And then it was time for them to sing.

As they began the tearjerker ballad, everyone could see it was going to be a fantastic performance. Mickey played the piano while Dan and Greg sat on stools on the stage.

Louis was singing along quietly, and Tulisa looked very impressed. Nicole even wiped a tear from her eye. It was a very emotional performance – full of heart.

And when it was over, the crowd went wild.

'You stripped everything back,' said Tulisa, once the cheers died down. 'It was just three lovely, good-looking lads, singing beautiful harmonies, with a great song choice. This is when I love you the most. My favourite performance as of yet!'

The boys were absolutely overjoyed. Dan was lost in his own world as he looked up to the sky and mouthed 'Thank you'.

'Guys, great to see you back where you were when we chose you to be in the finals,' said Gary, smiling. 'Great vocally, great song choice!'

But he got huge boos from the audience when he added: 'One thing for me, if I'm sitting in a record label right now, looking for the next big boy band, is it you guys? I don't think it is – there's something that's slightly dated about this band.'

No one could understand what Gary was saying. They'd sung beautifully, they were sweet, funny, sexy boys – what on earth could be missing?

But then he said something that would crush the boys. 'There's something that's just not got the edge that Union J has – I don't know what it is.'

'They've got the vocals,' said Tulisa, defending the talented trio.

'They *have* got the vocals and I feel bad for saying that,' replied Gary – but the damage was already done.

Nicole was still struggling to compose herself after the beautiful performance. It had affected her so deeply she had been crying, and her voice cracked when she tried to give her opinion.

'I don't know what Gary's talking about because you just brought tears to my eyes,' said the normally bubbly brunette. 'First of all, I love this song – thank you for choosing it. It has a deep personal meaning for me right now, so thank you so much for sharing it.'

It really was a personal moment for Nicole. Her beloved grandmother had died that week and she had flown back to America to attend the funeral. The words of the song – which are a letter to a loved one who passes away – had really struck a chord with how she felt. She finished by telling the boys she'd loved the arrangement and congratulated them on a job well done.

Louis was very happy with his District 3 boys. They had truly done him proud. 'Guys, this is what you do best – you're a brilliant vocal harmony group,' he said. 'Gary, what could you not like about that? It was simple, they were in tune…'

But Gary just sighed. 'I'm forced to compare them to Union J,' he said, being as honest as he could. 'And Union J just have the edge.'

There was definitely room for two new boy bands in the world and the boys had to remind themselves that everyone is entitled to their own opinion. They knew that the thousands of screaming fans outside their hotel day and night would think very differently to Gary.

But there was only room for one *X Factor* winner, and at some point, everyone would have to decide between the two groups. It seemed that Gary had already made his mind up.

'Guys, you worked so hard,' Louis continued. 'That so worked! I know the public are going to vote for you, and keep you here next week.'

Dermot O'Leary took over the reins from the judges and said: 'Well done for upsetting Nicole with that song choice, naughty Louis!'

Then he turned to the boys. 'You got slammed the last couple of weeks, so you've got to be happier this week,' he said.

'Yeah, definitely,' declared Mickey, on behalf of the group.

'And to be fair, Gary is splitting hairs as well…' Dermot added.

'Of course you're going to compare us,' said Mickey, bravely. 'We understand that, but we're different in that they are more pop and we're more RnB pop.'

The boys all agreed, and backstage, the Union J boys were almost certainly agreeing, too.

Afterwards, the boys went on Twitter and said: 'Hopefully we gave you the performance you've been waiting for, so now we need U 3eeks to pick up the phone and vote'.

All they could do now was wait.

DID YOU KNOW?

Greg loves profiteroles, and he's the only one in the band who is in a relationship. Sorry girls, he's taken!

On Sunday morning, District 3 woke up feeling very serious.

They tweeted: 'Always loved & never forgotten. Bravery & Courage. Lest we forget. #RemembranceSunday'.

At 11am, they held a two-minute silence − as did all the other acts − in support of our country's fallen soldiers. It was a poignant day and the boys were especially pleased that not one of their '3eeks' had posted during those two minutes.

'No one on my timeline tweeted in them 2 minutes! #proud', they tweeted afterwards.

Later on, they looked out of the window and saw a group of fans, dedicated and patient, waiting to meet them. They'd already done a 'meet and greet' for the day so they didn't have time to go down and see them. Instead they tweeted them, saying: 'Girls outside… We saw you! Love ya! Thanks for the support'.

And they must have felt incredibly supported, because today was the day when their Twitter followers reached a huge 300,000!

Even Niall from One Direction, who had been so supportive of the boys, tweeted the numbers to vote for the boys to encourage his own fans to share the love, saying: 'Help @District3music to get through and vote.'

The seconds slowly ticked by − the boys had no idea that tonight would bring the biggest battle of the show so far. And as they travelled to the studio for the results show, the nerves really began to kick in.

Together with the other acts, Greg Dan and Mickey performed U2's anthem 'Beautiful Day', but as much as they enjoyed it, they were really just waiting for Dermot O'Leary to announce the results of last night's competition.

And finally, it was time.

As Dermot started to reel off the names, the boys began to feel sick with nerves.

UNION J AND DISTRICT 3: BATTLE OF THE BANDS

'James, Rylan, Jahmene, Ella…'

There were only three names left to call and just one place for them to win.

'It's now down to just District 3, Union J and Christopher,' said Dermot, nervously. 'Only one act is certain of a place. The final act returning next week is… Christopher!'

District 3 were devastated – this was the last thing they wanted. They knew that the country had been divided over voting for both boy bands, who they had taken into their hearts equally. But now one of them would have to go and they had just a few minutes of singing to prove that it shouldn't be them.

'I can't believe how incredibly tense this is for you,' said Dermot. 'In just a few minutes you'll have to battle it out in the sing-off, and the judges will have to decide who stays and who's going home.'

District 3 were up first and as Dermot wished them luck, they went off to prepare.

Louis looked gutted. How would he choose between the bands? They were both his acts, he'd mentored them for months now.

'Okay, guys,' he said. 'They're going to sing their hearts out, this means so much to them – everybody get ready for District 3!'

They started singing Bruno Mars' 'Just The Way You Are' and although clearly upset and nervous, the boys really did sing their hearts out. You could hear their voices wobble with emotion. It was only natural – this was the most important moment of their lives.

When they finished, they gave the Union J boys a huge hug. Everyone knew that there could only be one winner tonight and it wasn't anyone's fault.

They'd done everything they could. All they could do now was wait for Union J to finish singing and as they listened to their rivals performing, they could hear how amazing they sounded.

It would be down to the judges to decide.

Dermot went to Louis first.

But the mentor looked devastated and insisted: 'No way am I sending ether of these acts home, I can't do it. No way!'

Louis was adamant – he simply wouldn't vote.

'So we have to go with a majority vote from the other judges,' said Dermot, and turned to Gary.

'Okay, when I saw both these acts in the bottom two I thought this was going to be quite simple, actually,' he said. 'Because in the past District 3 have always sang really well in this competition so I thought in a sing-off they would beat these guys easily.

'The shame is,' he continued, 'tonight that was one of your worst vocal performances to date – I'm so disappointed.'

He then told Union J that although they had less harmonies than the District 3 boys, he felt they wanted it more.

'This means the act I'm sending home tonight is District 3. Sorry, guys.'

The boys looked gutted. And to be fair, so did Union J. George even shook his head as if trying to shake a nightmare away. It wasn't nice for any of them.

Nicole was next. 'You know what, District 3? For you, having a bad day of harmonies is other people having a good day with their harmonies,' she told them. 'So you should be very proud of that – you've got my heart, you really do.'

But Nicole's kind words did nothing to soothe the boys' worries.

'The group that I think is a more mature group, and a little bit more ready for this right now is…'

Greg put his arms round his bandmates.

'…Union J. I'm so sorry, guys.'

So District 3 were going home. Union J had won the Battle of the Bands and for Greg, Dan and Mickey their *X Factor* journey was over.

The boys went over to Josh, JJ, George and Jaymi and all seven lads hugged each other tightly. It must have been so hard to hold it together on stage when all they wanted to do was cry.

'Tulisa, who would you have gone with?' asked Dermot.

Her opinion didn't matter at this stage but everyone wanted to know who she would have voted to keep.

'I think that their performances were amazing in different ways,' she said. 'Like they say, one is a vocal harmony band, the other a more kind of commercial boy band. I have a deep connection with them, so I would have saved District 3.'

It was great to know that at least one of the judges had wanted them to stay in the competition, but it meant nothing.

Now it was time for them to say their goodbyes.

'It's the most gutting feeling in the world,' said Greg. 'I just want to say a massive thank you to everyone, everyone backstage, everyone who's made this experience life changing for me.'

Dan said: 'Thank you to the judges for even letting us take part in the competition – I'm so grateful.'

Gary clapped and looked very sad, while Tulisa could hardly look at the camera at all.

The audience was shown a montage of all the boys' best bits – from auditions to Bootcamp, to the live shows. It was very emotional and Greg had tears in his eyes as he relived his journey.

Louis joined them on stage and Dermot asked what went wrong. 'Nothing went wrong at all,' he said. 'They just didn't get enough votes. I hope they get a record deal, they're a readymade pop act.'

But Dermot pressed him: why didn't they get enough votes?

'I really don't know,' he replied, clearly confused. 'Maybe having the two boy bands was splitting the vote. But they're brilliant guys to work with, they're a dream.'

Mickey smiled and laughed as Dermot went on to ask what their best moment had been.

'Performing every Saturday night has been the most phenomenal feeling,' said Greg. 'And we hope it's not the last of us.'

Dan added: 'And also the friendships we've made with all the contestants and backstage – like James, I absolutely love him!'

The boys would be back together with the other acts very soon – at the *X Factor* 2012 tour – but for now, it was time to leave the stage. The crowds cheered them one last time.

DID YOU KNOW?

Greg and his sister once fell down in front of the whole of Colchester's town centre when it was icy. Cringe!

Later that evening, the country was buzzing with talk of the Battle of the Boy Bands climactic ending. After so many rumours of bitter rivalry, District 3 were determined to set the record straight.

UNION J AND DISTRICT 3: BATTLE OF THE BANDS

It had been an epic battle, they admitted, but only musically – in actual fact they were great friends.

It must have been so hard for both bands to want to beat the other so badly on the live shows while spending so much time together as friends for the rest of the week. Living in the hotel meant they got to spend a lot of time together and had grown close.

'There's been this whole thing in the press about us being rivals,' Greg told *The Xtra Factor*. 'But to be honest we've made the best friendship, and I wish them all the luck in the world.'

He'd seen it coming and had a sneaking feeling it was their time to leave, but there was no bitterness and Dan even said: 'Union J are amazingly talented guys and they are friends of ours, so they deserve it.'

The Battle of the Bands might have been over but in their hearts, there had never been a battle between the boys.

Union J's Josh was quick to agree. 'When they told us we were through, we were like "yes!" but then two seconds later, you realise that District 3 are heartbroken at the same time and you go and comfort them.'

And comfort them they did, with hugs and smiles.

James Arthur was also gutted that District 3 had left. He'd thought that he was the one who would be sent home after having a terrible feeling that something bad would happen that night. 'Thankfully it wasn't me,' he told Caroline. 'But when we lost our mates, District 3, I was really disappointed.'

Louis was the most shocked to see the two bands battling it out in the bottom two, especially as they were both his acts.

'I thought both groups were big enough and good enough to have different fan bases,' he admitted.

It seems that Union J fans had good taste as they were District 3 fans, too – and District 3 fans were just as discerning, because they were Union J fans as well! All over the country they must have been struggling to decide who out of their two favourites to vote for. After all, who could possibly decide between them both?

Tulisa told the presenters that she was shocked that both boys were in the bottom two, while Louis said he really wasn't happy that they'd had to battle it out.

Greg definitely had the last word, though. 'Although it's the end of the competition, it's the start for us as a band.'

And it certainly was.

The day after the boys' sad exit, Greg, Dan and Mickey appeared on the *Daybreak* sofa with Lorraine Kelly and gave all their fans the news they had been desperate to hear: they weren't going anywhere!

Greg said: 'We've had the most amazing time, and we've made some great friends – it's just the start for us.'

When Lorraine suggested it had been a great platform for the band, Greg added: 'Yeah, of course – we couldn't have asked for anything better. It's allowed us to create an amazing fan base. Now we just need to get back on writing the album and doing lots of gigs.'

Dan hinted at how much hard work the trio had put in when he said it would be good to 'catch up on some sleep'. It wasn't surprising – I bet they couldn't wait to wake up in their own beds!

The boys promised that if they got the chance, they would go along to the remaining live shows to support their new friends and would vote for the rest of the contestants.

Caroline Flack, who joined them on the *This Morning* sofa, gave Dan some hope that he might have a chance with Ella

Henderson, by revealing she didn't think the teen songstress and Union J's George Shelley were romantically involved.

'There seems to be photographers following them around in the dark, looking for any movement that could be considered a relationship,' said Caroline. 'I personally don't think that they're in a relationship. She tells me they're not in a relationship – I just think they are really close friends.'

The next day, photos emerged in the *Daily Mail* that showed how popular the boys had been with the other contestants. Rylan and Ella were seen cuddling up to each other, watching with despair as District 3 were kicked off the show. In fact, Rylan even had to wipe a tear from his face as the realisation that his new friends would have to leave suddenly dawned on him.

James Arthur was also seen with his head in his hands, while Christopher Maloney was so shocked, he covered his mouth with his hands. They could hardly bear to watch!

But caught up in a whirlwind of media attention, District 3 were feeling positive about the future – and shared their plans to make up for lost dating time.

'We have been in this *X Factor* bubble for ages and we have never really had the opportunity to go out much,' Greg told the *Sun*. He revealed that while they'd been on the show there was a strict rule to stay away from girls as much as possible, and since they were all single, it was very tough, especially with so many pretty girls wanting to get to know them.

'Obviously we are keeping focused and professional – this is our career that we have to think about – but if a sexy lady threw herself at us, we would be straight on it.'

It was the piece of news that cheered up devastated District 3 fans all over the country – and made them very excited about what was in store for them as fans.

DISTRICT 3

A few weeks later it was clear that despite not being in *The X Factor* anymore, District 3's star was still rising. Since their shock exit, they had been filmed out and about in London almost every day. They even went to see Amelia Lily in *Shrek* for Children In Need, and got a lot of attention from their fans afterwards. Jumping into a rickshaw to take them back to their hotel, the lads laughed and joked about as a mountain of girls tried to pile in with them. By the smiles on their faces, everyone could tell they were very much still living the dream.

The lads are extremely hopeful about the future. They cite One Direction as their inspiration, the band who came third in *The X Factor* 2010 and have been more successful than anyone dreamed of. 'To have even one percent of 1D's success would be absolutely amazing,' Mickey told the *Sun*.

We reckon they'll have a much bigger share than that...